PRACTICAL JEWELLERY REPAIR

Practical Jewellery Repair

James E. Hickling

N. A. G. Press Ltd
Ipswich, Suffolk

First Published in 1987

Copyright © James E. Hickling,
and N.A.G. Press Ltd, 1987

Illustrations by Des Howard

ACKNOWLEDGEMENTS
The 'Jewellers' Guide to Gemstone Handling',
which appears in the book as Appendix 3, is rep-
roduced by kind permission of Howard Rubin,
gemologist for Leer Gems Ltd, importers of
precious stones, of New York, USA.

British Library Cataloguing in Publication
Data

  Hickling, James Ernest
    Practical jewellery repair.
    1. Jewelry—Repair--Amateurs' manuals
    I. Title
    739.27'6 TS740

  ISBN 0-7198-0082-X

Typeset by Budget Typesetting, Beckenham,
Kent. Printed and bound in Great Britain by
Anchor Brendon Ltd, Tiptree, Colchester,
Essex.

Contents

To my son, Steven
to make up for his
inadequate apprenticeship

.

Introduction

As nearly all jewellery is purely ornamental, its quality is judged mainly on appearance. If it looks good it is good. This makes jewellery repairing rather an inexact craft: it does not matter a lot how you achieve the result so long as it looks good. Not so the poor watch repairer whose efforts are judged solely by the accuracy of the timekeeping. The gleaming results of his efforts are hidden away and his slightest mistake is betrayed by the position of two hands on a dial. With him there is a right and a wrong way of doing everything and for him a textbook has to be precise and imper sonal.

For the jewellery repairer, the ideal is the repair that cannot be detected. The means of achieving that result is largely immaterial, so a textbook for him is more of a personal guide book showing the shortcuts and avoiding the pitfalls. Each person's talent, imagination, co-ordination and even eyesight are different so when I have found the best way of doing a job others have probably found a different way. For this reason I have allowed myself the privilege of using the first person singular. I can answer any critics by the comment 'I did not say it was the right way or the only way, just my way'.

I apologise for the mixture of Imperial and metric measurements, I don't believe I am more confused and confusing than anyone else. I ordered some ½ inch copper tube recently and was proudly informed by the plumbers' merchant that they had now gone metric and I would have to have 15 mm tube - how many *feet* did I want?

Chapter 1

Workshop Layout and Equipment

A lot of jewellery repair work could be carried out on a kitchen table and the ideal would probably be three largish rooms each with running water, power, light and ventilation. A reasonable compromise would be one large room with a porcelain sink, good lighting and ventilation and two or three power points.

The layout of such a workshop would be largely dictated by the position of the facilities. The layout in Fig. 1-1 is given as a general guide. Here are a few points to watch out for:

Gilding and silverplating involve the use of heated cyanide solutions so these should be close to the sink and ventilation, preferably an extractor fan with a hood. Porcelain is specified for the sink because stainless steel does not always live up to its reputation when in contact with these chemicals. Sulphuric and any other acid should be kept well away from the cyanide as the combination of these two produces a gas similar to that used in execution chambers!

Securing the Vice Bench

The bench carrying the vice, which will be used mainly for drawing down wire, should be well fixed to the wall and floor. As most jewellers need a safe of some description, it will serve a dual purpose if it can be built into the bench beneath the vice. It will be a heavy anchorage better than most wall plugs, which tend to leave their moorings under the constant punishment wire drawing exerts on them. Be sure to leave plenty of clear space in front of the vice and no sharp projections opposite. It takes a good deal of energy to draw down even a 1 mm (0.04 in) diameter piece of wire and if it breaks unexpectedly you will shoot backwards a couple of yards before you regain your balance.

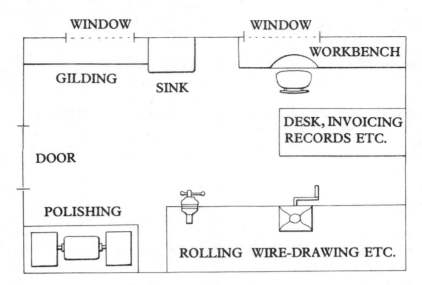

Fig. 1-1 The workshop layout depends to a large extent of the space available. This has been found a practical layout for a working jeweller. The equipment near the sink needs an efficient ventilator and so does the polishing equipment. The bench shown at the bottom must be substantial and very firmly anchored to the floor and wall.

It is best to have the polishing motor mounted on a bench by itself as the vibrations set up when the machine is in use cause everything else on that bench to work its way to the edge and over the side. For this reason the dust boxes, which can be homemade from plywood, should have a beading round the top edges to prevent work placed on them dropping over the side (Fig 1-2). A worthwhile extra is some form of extractor fan mounted below the box covering the polishing mop. Without it, the dust mounts up on every flat surface in the room at a disheartening rate. It need not be expensive or elaborate, a small induction motor-driven fan mounted below a quarter inch mesh net and exhausting into an old pillow case works quite well. An old vacuum cleaner can be used for this purpose, but it takes strong nerves to put up with the noise.

The ideal polishing motor is the double-ended high-speed induction motor used in the dental trade. These machines are completely sealed so that no dust or abrasive can get inside the works. They are very smooth running and almost silent - but also expensive.

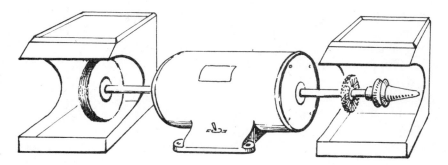

Fig. 1-2 A double-ended high-speed polishing machine, which should be mounted on a separate bench with beading round the edge to prevent work from falling to the floor.

A less expensive version supplied by most jewellery tool dealers works just as well, but you have to put up with the whine and see that the ventilation slots do not become clogged with fluff. These machines must be fixed down to the bench.

Though the ideal polishing speed is about 3000 rpm, an ordinary induction motor working at 1475 rpm, such as an old ½ horse power washing machine motor will do the work; but it takes longer and the mops wear out a lot faster.

The Jeweller's Workbench

The jeweller's workbench should be about 3 ft (95 cm) in height but, depending on the size of the jeweller, this could vary an inch or so either way. This is often compensated for by having a stool with adjustable height, but as the adjustment usually relies on a screw thread, the stool has an unpleasant habit of slowly creeping up or down, which is not noticed until you have been working at the bench for an hour and developed a stiff neck or a mysterious ache in the shoulders, which can spoil your concentration at a crucial moment.

The workbench in Fig. 1-3 has two bench pegs. A bench peg is a wedge shaped piece of wood, usually beech, traditionally used by jewellers as a mini-bench. It was jammed into a slot in the side of the bench. In this case, the centre one is for filing against and is made of wood; hardwood lasts longer. The one on the left is cut from ⅛ in (3mm) thick aluminium sheet and pivots on the fixing screw so that it can be moved out of the way when not in use. This is used to support sheet material while being cut with a piercing saw. It can be made from other materials, but aluminium is sufficiently rigid and least damaging to saw blades. Left-handed jewellers should have it fitted to the right hand side of the bench - or have an inexhaustable supply of saw blades.

Filings and clippings drop into the recess below the pegs. For this reason it has a sloping lip to prevent loss. Traditionally jewellers have used what they call a 'skin', a large piece of soft leather slung beneath the semicircular hole to catch the filings, etc. This has two drawbacks: if a heavy tool is dropped into it, the filings fly into the air, taking to the four winds, and if a red hot signet ring should slip from the tweezers, it does not stop until it hits the jeweller's thighs.

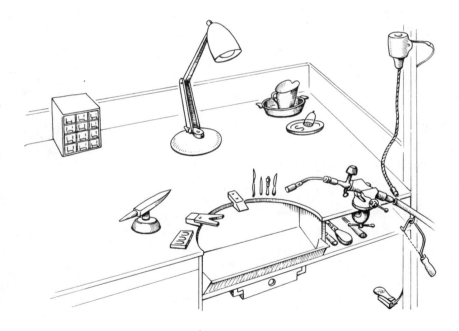

Fig. 1-3 A workbench layout that differs slightly from the truly tradition design. There is a wooden box, instead of the usual skin, to catch filings, etc, below which a drawer is fitted. There is a peg for sawing as well as one for filing and the torch can be held in the vice as shown so that both hands can be used to hold parts together when soldering.

There is a ready-made alternative in galvanized steel with handy tool racks around the sides and a wire gauze circle in the centre, through which the filings pass to be caught in a removable can beneath. It serves the purpose very well, but is noisy in use and is vulnerable to Bakers Fluid, used in soldering. Also, any hot gemstone accidentally dropped in it inevitably comes into contact with cold metal which can be disastrous for the stone.

Veneered Bench Top

The wooden container illustrated in Fig. 1-3 overcomes these disadvantages and is easy to make oneself. It has the added advantage that a very convenient drawer can be fitted beneath it. It should be varnished so that the filings are easy to sweep up and the corners should be rounded with wood filler. The bench top in the illustration is ¾ in (18mm) thick chipboard covered with mahogany veneer, which can be bought in 6 ft by 2 ft (2 m by 0.75 m) sheets ready to varnish. It looks and feels more professional than plain or painted timber and one is more inclined to keep it clean and tidy to preserve the feeling.

The wooden surround should be at least 6 in (15cm) high. Small stones flick out of the tweezers with annoying frequency and it is far easier to search for them on the bench than on the floor beneath.

The semi-circular cut-out should be 20 in wide by 8 in (50 cm by 20 cm) deep. The pan bottom to bench top distance should be about 8 in (20 cm), and front to back of the pan about 10 in (25 cm) to accommodate the longest tools used.

The floor covering in a jeweller's workshop is important as a lot of precious metal and stones eventually find their way there. A medium to light grey seems to provide the least camouflage for stones and gold. As to bare floorboards - I once had the pleasure of cleaning up a workshop that had been used for jewellery repair and manufacture for more than 70 years and so much treasure was found in the cracks between the floorboards that it was deemed economical to lift them to recover what had passed right through before the cracks had become clogged. After that, no corner was left unprodded and even the outside window ledges rendered a selection of snippings, so heaven knows what must have ended up in the street over the years. It was not uncommon in the past for the wooden floors of old jewellery workshops to be auctioned for the lemel (precious metal filings) they contained.

So a light grey P.V.C. floor covering is a justifiable expense - unless you want to use the floorboards as a supplement to your old age pension.

Some workshops have a pickle bench and sometimes a treadle-operated brass wire scratch brush. The former usually consists of a lead-covered bench with a raised lip all round on which stand a cast iron gas ring, earthenware pot of sulphuric acid, another pot of clean water, and a copper pickling pan. The pickling pan is used to scoop acid from the pot and is then placed on the gas ring and heated. Items of jewellery that have been oxidized by heating are dropped bodily into the acid or, when this is not possible, the oxidized parts only are dipped into it then rinsed in the clean water.

The only advantage of heating the acid is that the pickling or de-oxidizing action is almost instantaneous, whereas cold acid can take five to ten minutes to do the same work. The disadvantages are many. Apart from the space taken up by the bench, the fumes that escape into the workshop are corrosive and attack any metal they come into contact with and a quick whiff is guaranteed to give you a sore throat. In addition, the acid reacts with the copper pan to create green crystals which rapidly spread all over the bench and eventually over the lead lip and on to the clothes. If it is not noticed and dealt with at the time, a white patch appears on the clothing which quickly becomes a hole.

Siting the Acid

With so much against it, I can never understand how this method came into being. A much cleaner and more convenient way of using the acid is to have a Pyrex tumbler or jug containing the acid standing in a wide shallow bowl of clean water and placed at the back of the workbench as shown in Fig. 1-3. The items to be pickled are suspended from the edge of the tumbler on a short length of silver wire, or in the case of a lot of small items, such as earwires, placed on a piece of perforated silver sheet and lowered to the bottom. The back of an old silver pocket watch case with a loop of wire soldered to it is ideal. A few holes can be stamped into it with a scriber to allow the acid to drain away when removing it from the tumbler.

I specified Pyrex for the tumbler because, when the acid is initially diluted, a considerable amount of heat is generated, sufficient sometimes to crack a coffee jar or other ordinary glass container.

A word of warning is appropriate here: when diluting acid *always pour the acid into the water*, never the reverse. To do it the wrong way round is like throwing cold, wet chips into hot boiling fat - a minor explosion occurs. A way of remembering which way round to do it is to substitute the word PAW for POUR: Pour Acid into Water. The proportions are roughly one of acid to ten of water.

I remember wondering how many tools I would ruin by having a bowl of acid on the workbench, but if the bench is as solid as it should be, remarkably little escapes the water bowl surrounding it. With an absorbent tissue on an old plate close to the bowl for drying the items on, even the water does not drip anywhere. As long as the water is changed often enough to prevent it becoming too contaminated with acid, it can do little damage.

The treadle scratchbrush with its drip feed of cleaning fluid was a boon when silver charm bracelets were at the height of fashion. I know of no quicker or harmless way of brightening them up after pickling. With ten or twenty of these to do at a time the space taken up by the bench was justified. But now their popularity has waned, a hand brush used with detergent and water is usually adequate for the few items such as trace necklets that cannot be given a polished finish.

Tools and Equipment

Basic hand tools required for a workshop:
  2 pairs of flat-nosed pliers
  1 pair of round-nosed pliers
  1 pair of flat- topped snips
  1 pair of ring pliers
  1 pair of tin shears
  1 half of round 6 in (15 cm) ring maker's file. Cut 2
  1 triblet
  1 size stick
  2 pairs of tweezers
  3 needle files; rat-tail, double half-round, knife edge
  3 broaches, different sizes
  1 saw frame, 2 grades of blade
  3 gravers; square, round bottom, chisel

1 hammer
1 mallet
1 ring clamp
graining and mill graining tools
1 set of finger sizes
1 scriber
1 set watchmaker's screwdrivers
1 penknife
1 pin vice
1 brass wire brush
draw plate and tongs
propane torch
ruler, slide gauge and micrometer
eyeglass
asbestos block
emery paper
polishing paper

That is a basic kit of handtools and there are very few jobs you could not tackle with them. Any additional tools are for speed, convenience and ease of working.

Pliers come with two types of joint. One is the box joint, as shown in Fig. 1-4 where - by some mysterious method no-one has been able to explain to me - one arm is threaded through the other as illustrated. The other is the lap joint used in most hinged tools. The box joint is far superior and longer lasting and withstands the constant twisting action jewellery work subjects it to. If the handles are plain or plated metal, grip lines filed across them will prevent them slipping when the hands get a little sweaty.

There are many types of cheap pliers available and it should not

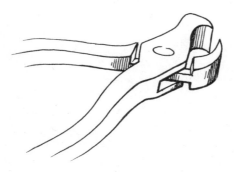

Fig. 1-4 Pliers with a box joint, where one arm passes through the other, should always be chosen in preference to ones hinged like scissors. Those shown are cutters.

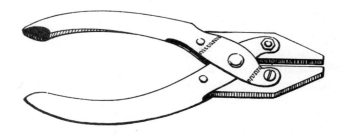

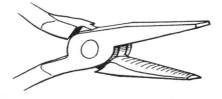

Fig. 1-5 On the left are ring pliers. One jaw is rounded for gripping ring-shaped pieces. On the right are parallel jaw pliers for gripping parts with parallel sides without a wedging action.

go against the grain to pay maybe five times the price for an item that looks identical but is a much better tool that will last a lifetime and be a pleasure to use. Cheap ones can be brittle and break easily at the base of the jaw if too much pressure is put on them; too soft so that the tips bend and will not grip properly; too stiff so that the little finger aches from having to force them open; or too loose so the jaws slip out of alignment when in use. This applies to flat-nosed and round-nosed pliers and particularly to flat topped snips. Unless the cutting edges are properly hardened they will become useless in no time. Even good ones should only be used for cutting non-ferrous metals.

The tin shears are not so critical. They are used mainly for cutting sheet solder into small squares, which puts little strain on them.

Ring pliers (Fig. 1-5) have one flat jaw and one round jaw and are used for gripping and bending rings or other items of similar diameter. The ready made item, being a specialist tool of limited demand, is rather expensive. It is not a difficult task to grind one

11

jaw of a suitable pair of flat-nosed pliers to the desired shape. The same illustration shows parallel-jaw pliers - another specialist tool, to hold flat items without squeezing them into a taper or allowing them to slip.

The ring maker's file differs from an ordinary half round file in that it is more slender over the whole length to enable it to be used on the inside of small finger rings.

The triblet (sometimes called a tapered mandrel) is a 10 in (25cm) length of case hardened steel, approximately ⅜ in (10mm) at the narrow end and ⅞ in (22mm) at the other, plus the handle. It is mainly used for hammering rings into shape after they have had their sizes altered. If it is not hardened - and some are not - it will quickly become pitted with hammer marks. These marks will be transferred to the inside of every ring that is hammered over them, causing a lot of unneccessary filing and finishing work to remove them. To check, run a file gently over the surface, it should roll over, leaving hardly a mark. If the file bites at all, the triblet is not hardened.

The triblet (Fig. 1-6) is a solid steel tapered bar, incorporating a handle, on which rings can be shaped using a mallet. The size stick is very similar, but is a gauge marked with ring sizes, not a tool. As it will be in constant daily use, an aluminium one will wear very quickly. A stainless steel one will last indefinately. On new ones, the size markings are sometimes quite rough and should be smoothed down with fine emery to prevent scoring the inside of the rings.

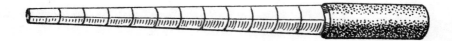

Fig. 1-6 A size (or sizing) stick. One made of stainless steel tube is best. Even plated ones are better than those made of aluminium, which wear very quickly.

Cheap AA grade tweezers are all that is needed; they are mainly used for gripping work that is being soldered and they soon become softened and distorted at the tips and require frequent filing to reshape them. An additional type of tweezers, shown in Fig. 1-7 is often useful however. The tips are bent at 45 degrees as shown.

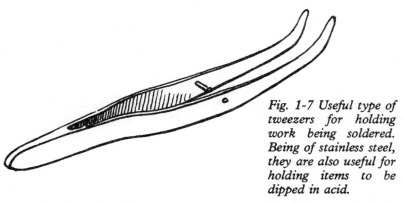

Fig. 1-7 Useful type of tweezers for holding work being soldered. Being of stainless steel, they are also useful for holding items to be dipped in acid.

They are made from stainless steel. The bend enables certain jobs to be gripped comfortably where straight tweezers would cause the hands to be held at an awkward angle and being stainless they are useful for holding items that require only a dip in the acid.

Many shapes of needle file are available and can be acquired as the need arises, but the three mentioned will cover most work. The knife edge file is used to shape up the tips of claw settings. In use, the broad edge rests against the surface of the gemstone, so it should be perfectly smooth to avoid damaging the stone. New ones will usually be found to have a rough prominent edge as shown at the top in Fig. 1-8. This should be removed with carborundum stone and polished with emery paper.

Broaches are five-sided tapered needles. One held in a pin vice is used for enlarging the inside diameter of tube and small rings. They are indispensable when fitting new hinges to watch cases or brooches. They break easily but are reasonably cheap, so three would be the bare minimum.

Two types of saw frame are available. One is adjustable and the other (Fig. 1-9) has a fixed frame. As all saw blades for jewellery work are more or less the same length and relatively cheap, there is no point in having an adjustable frame, which is heavier and more cumbersome than the fixed frame.

The two grades of blade are 2/0 and 4/0. The first is the heavier and for general purposes; the finer one is for cutting very thin sheet and cleaning out cracks before soldering.

A great variety of gravers is available but as a jeweller uses them mainly for stone setting and matching up bits of decoration, the three listed will suffice. A graver can be made by grinding a broken

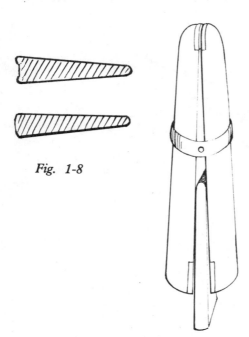

Fig. 1-8

Fig. 1-8 Some needle files have an edge like that at the top, shown in section, which can damage gems when filing metal around them. The edge should be stoned smooth and square as shown in the lower sketch.

Fig. 1-12 A ring clamp, which will hold a ring firmly for working on it. The clamp is designed for holding in the hand, but can be held in a vice if the craftsman is careful. It has two wooden parts with leather jaws (at the top) which clamp the ring when the wedge at the other end is tapped in.

needle file to shape if necessary.

A good general purpose grade of emery paper is Oakley's 1M. It comes in sheets 9 by 11 in (23 by 28 cm). The best way of using it is to cut it in half lengthways and wrap one strip round a 10 in (25 cm) length of ¾ by ¼ in (20 by 6 mm) wood, each fold should be scored with a penknife as shown in Fig.1-10 so that strips can be easily torn off as they become worn. The paper is held in place by a drawing pin or adhesive tape. The other strip of emery is wrapped around a piece of ⅜ in (10 mm) dowel and secured in the same way. This is for cleaning up the inside of rings.

Polishing paper is grade 4/0 emery and is used for getting a fine polish on steel and platinum.

The hammer should be a 2 oz one of the type shown in Fig.1-11. One I recently bought from a large jewellery tool supplier had a handle out of all proportion to the head and the round end forced into the rectagular hole in the hammer head, the gaps being filled with epoxy resin. It sported a Union Jack sticker with the words: Better buy...British tools. In the circumstances I couldn't decide whether this was a threat or a recommendation, so I suggest you buy that item from a shop where you can see what you are getting.

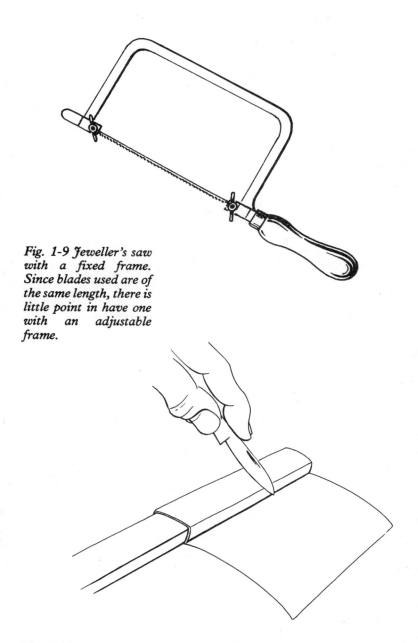

Fig. 1-9 Jeweller's saw with a fixed frame. Since blades used are of the same length, there is little point in have one with an adjustable frame.

Fig. 1-10 Fixing some emery paper to make an emery stick. Scoring the paper makes it easy to tear off worn strips.

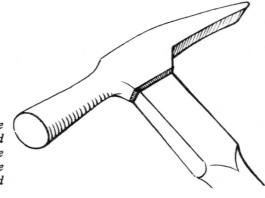

Fig. 1-11 A two-ounce forged hammer head with a cross-pean at one end. Make sure that the head is firmly and neatly fixed.

The mallet should be 9 or 10 in (about 25cm) long with a hide or plastic head.

Ring clamps are only used occasionally, so the wooden variety with a wedge, shown in Fig. 1-12, to close them are adequate.

Graining tools are sold in 60 mm lengths of 2.5mm diameter hardened steel (Fig. 1-13). They are tapered at one end to various diameters with the tip made concave. You can buy them in sets of ten in a box complete with handle. This is the best way initially, but the smaller sizes wear out much quicker than the larger ones so it is cheaper to buy individual sizes subsequently. They are used for pushing the small nobs or 'grains' of metal over gemstones when setting.

Mill graining tools (Fig. 1-14) are minute steel wheels with a series of round indentations around the periphery and are fitted, free to rotate, in the end of a short length of steel rod. Capped by an ordinary graver handle, they are used to put the finishing touches to a 'mill grained' setting. Unless they are kept lightly oiled, the wheels quickly rust solid. A fine, medium and coarse grade will be needed.

A set of fingers sizes (Fig. 1-15) will be needed even if you are not taking the customer's finger size personally, because there are many occasions when after a ring's size has been altered that it cannot be made perfectly round. An example is when the head is too thick to bend, or bending might distort the settings. As the finished size cannot be checked on the ring stick, the only way of ascertaining whether it is the correct size is by fitting it on one of your own fingers and measuring the size of that finger which the ring fits.

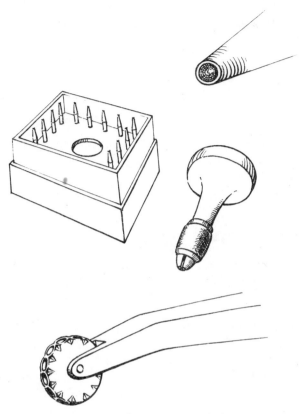

Fig. 1-13 (Top) Graining tools in a boxed set of different sizes. They have hollow ends as shown at top right. One held in the handle provided can be pushed into metal to raise a bead for setting small gems.
Fig. 1-14 (Above) A mill graining tool for making a row of very small beads or grains in soft metal by rolling the wheel across the surface. It is used for decoration and for finishing mill-grained settings. Three different sizes are normally required.

A set of watchmaker's screwdrivers (Fig. 1-16) is needed for the removal of watch movements from cases in order to work on the case and the occasional spectacle frame repair where the lenses have to be removed first.

A pin vice, such as Eclipse size 121 as shown in Fig. 1-17, will do most of the work such as holding brooches or gripping earwires while filing a safety groove, but the two larger sizes come in handy on occasion.

The brass wire brush (Fig. 1-18) is used as described earlier in

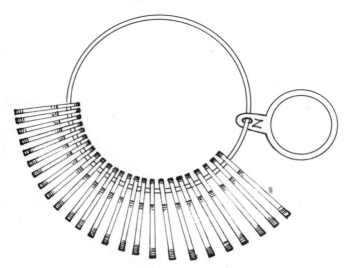

Fig. 1-15 A set of rings of graduated diameters called 'finger sizes' is essential for measuring finger sizes. The various scales are compared in the Appendix at the back of the book.

Fig. 1-16 Watchmakers' screwdrivers are needed for the occasional job involving a watch or a pair of spectacles.

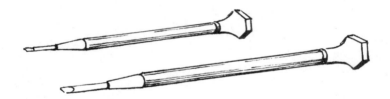

Fig. 1-17 A pin vice, which is hand-held and has a three-jaw chuck at one end to hold small work, particularly rod-shaped work.

this chapter. If the wood is untreated, it will warp if left wet and the bristles will fall out, so it is as well to wax or varnish the wood and keep it as dry as possible.

Fig. 1-18 Brass wire brush for cleaning metals. The handle should be varnished if unpolished.

The carbon block (Fig. 1-19) should be about 5 by 3 by 1 in (13 by 8 by 2.5cm) and is used for supporting items for soldering that cannot satisfactorily be held in tweezers, such as heavy charm bracelets. It is also used for casting small pieces of metal when one does not have a piece of the right section at hand. A cavity of the required length and section is cut into the surface and filled with bits of scrap. When heated, they will form into a ball and this is pressed into the cavity with the smooth flat end of a pair of tweezers. There are charcoal and compressed pumice blocks available that will do the job just as well but they are messy and tend to disintegrate rapidly. Traditionally an asbestos block is used.

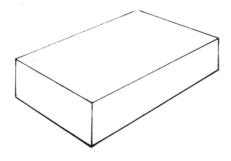

Fig. 1-19 Simple carbon block on which to rest parts when soldering and also for holding scrap for melting.

Ninety per cent of wire drawing can be carried out on one round hole drawplate (Fig. 1-20) with a range of holes between 0.06 in (1.5mm) and 0.02 in (0.5mm) diameter. You need to be something of a Hercules to draw down wire thicker than this without an expensive draw-bench. The same applies to shaped holes for D-section shank wire and square wire. Instead of buying a draw-bench, the money would be better spent on a set of rolls, such as those shown in Fig. 1-25. One other plate that is needed on rare occasions is a round hole one with diameters smaller than 0.02 in (0.5mm). Finer wires can be drawn down with a heavy pair of flat-nosed pliers, but thicker wires will require a pair of draw tongs (Fig. 1-21) whose handles are so shaped that as the pull increases the grip is tightened and the hook end of one handle prevents the hand from slipping off.

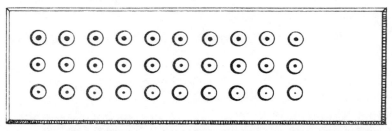

Fig. 1-20 Steel drawplate for wire drawing. The holes are tapered and in a series of sizes.

A 6 in (15 cm) stainless steel ruler with both imperial and metric markings is a great help in conversion for those with non- metric minds. The same can be said for a 6 in slide gauge (Fig. 1-22. Some very cheap ones are available and are sufficiently accurate, but if they are not stainless or plated the slightly acid sweat of one's hand quickly causes them to rust and become unreadable. The slide gauge is used mainly for measuring gemstones and settings and is far more convenient than a ruler.

The micrometer (Fig. 1-23) is used mainly for comparison measurements, e.g. matching a piece of wire or sheet to an existing piece. Even a cheap one is more accurate and easier to use for this purpose than a slide gauge.

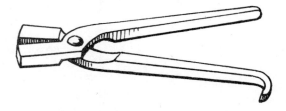

Fig. 1-21 Draw tongs for holding the end of a length of wire being pulled through a drawplate. The hook is needed when using a draw bench .

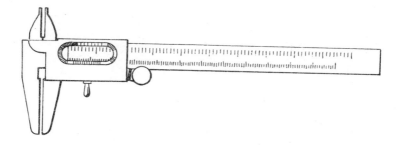

Fig. 1-22 (Top) A slide gauge, mainly used in jewellery work for measuring gems and gem settings. Usually it is a vernier gauge, which enables tenths of the smallest division on the main gauge to be measured.
Fig. 1-23 A micrometer, used for smaller measurements such as the diameter of wire or thickness of sheet. The end at the right, the thimble, is turned to open and close the jaws. The main scale is horizontal, along the barrel, and the fine scale around the thimble.

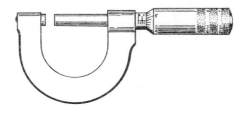

A 10x watchmaker's eyeglass will be necessary for examining the condition of small settings and a help in identifying gemstones. If your eyesight is such that you need some degree of magnification for all close work then a Binomag will be necessary. That illustrated in Fig. 1-24 has a focal length of about 5 in (12.5 cm) and will enable the user to judge distances accurately. It also avoids the strain of using only one eye as with an eyeglass.

The soldering torch has to be of a type that can be fixed to the bench, to leave the hands free to hold the work. Before the advent of natural gas the Birmingham Side-light was almost universally used by jewellers in the U.K. It was extremely versatile and had a pilot light. The gas department offered two alternatives which even together did not cover the range of the original. One was a mini-bunsen burner with a tiny compressor to give the flame

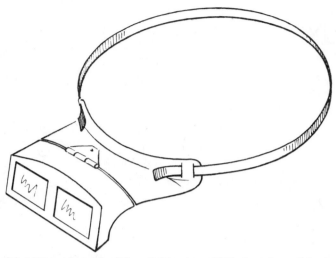

Fig. 1-24 A binocular magnifier of this type will be found much better than using an eyeglass in one eye. The headband holds it in front of the eyes and the magnifier can be hinged up out of the way when necessary. Some can be used when wearing spectacles.

greater intensity. The other was similar in appearance to the Birmingham Side-light but needed a constant supply of compressed air to operate it.

Eventually I gave them both away to people whose friendship I did not value too much and settled for a propane torch running on bottled gas as illustrated on the right in Fig. 1-3. I have seen various ingenious ways of fixing this to the bench but have found the swivelling vice with bench clamp, as shown in the illustration to be the most convenient. It gives lateral as well as up and down movement and the vice with its hammering pad has many other uses. I have always used a Sievert torch with the smallest jet, number 3537, and found it adequate for most repair work. For heavier work and for melting scrap I use jet numbers 3939 and 3941 respectively.

Machinery

The single most expensive piece of machinery in the jobbing jeweller's workshop would be the rolling mill. With the infinite range of materials available from bullion dealers it is possible to work without one, but it is very inconvenient and costly to keep a range of material large enough to cope with every job that comes along. It is up to the individual to weigh up the pros and cons and decide whether to profit the bullion dealer or court the bank manager.

The best set for the repairer would be that illustrated in Fig. 1-25. The main rolls are divided into halves, the plain half for rolling sheet and the other carrying a range of grooves for rolling a 7mm square rod by stages down to 1mm. There are extensions on the main rollers for fitting a variety of narrow rolls, the most useful being one for converting square wire into three different grades of half round.

There are cheaper sets on the market but they usually achieve the economy by fitting the handle directly to the rolls thus doing away with the step-down gearing. These usually come with two handles, one for each side, which implies it is a two-man job or you need biceps the size of the average person's thighs. Even with the advantage of the gears, it requires considerable strength to roll down 9ct. gold sheet much above 1mm thick and 20mm wide.

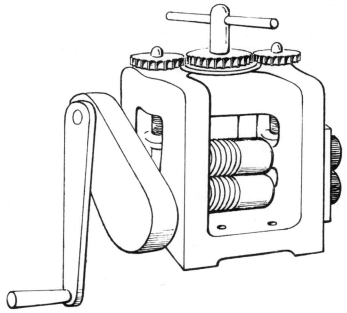

Fig. 1-25 A rolling mill is essential if the holding of costly stocks of many shapes of sheet and wires is to be avoided. It is like a steel mangle, fastened firmly to the bench. It is turned by a handle and the gap between the rolls can be adjusted from the top. The main rolls are divided into a plain section for rolling sheet and one with a range of grooves for round wire. Rolls for other shapes can be fitted.

Ring Sizing Machines

The first two ring sizing machines illustrated in Fig. 1-26 and Fig. 1-27 are those most commonly in use. The first is for enlarging gem rings and plain narrow wedding rings. The ring is placed over the central pillar and a roller of the appropriate profile fitted in position above the adjacent gear wheel. The handle is twisted clockwise causing the roller to close up against the ring shank and the gears to mesh. The handle is then moved from side to side around the central pivot and the pressure on the shank slowly increased, causing the shank to be stretched.

Its main drawback is that the more the shank is stretched, the thinner it becomes. This effect is not too noticeable up to one size, but above that the customer has cause to complain. (Almost the

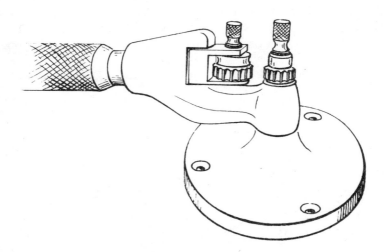

Fig. 1-26 One form of ring-sizing machine, used mainly for gem-set rings and plain wedding bands. Above the gears are two rollers; one can be changed to suit the ring. The ring is placed over the central post. Then the knurled handle on the arm, seen on the left, is rotated, which will cause the gears to move together and engage. Swinging the arm from side to side, while twisting the handle to increase the pressure, will squeeze the ring shank to stretch it.

same degree of enlargement can be achieved by placing the ring in the triblet and, keeping it pressed against the taper, subject the shank to a series of light hammer blows). So this piece of equipment is not essential, merely a time saver. If you decide to purchase one, check the set of rollers first. There are some on the market with about four usable rollers; the rest have been left to the imagination of an engineer and will not match any ring shank I have ever seen.

The second machine (Fig. 1-27) is used for enlarging rings of uniform thickness, which means mainly wedding rings. The vertical tapered part is split into four sections lengthways and these four sections are forced outwards when the lever is pressed down so that a ring placed on the taper will be enlarged (Fig. 1-28). They cope very well with 18ct and 22ct gold rings provided that any joins in the rings are well made. A poorly joined ring will quickly break, as will one that has not been annealed first. Also rings with a very deep hallmark tend to stretch more at the hallmark, which has caused a reduction in cross section at that point.

When stretching a ring with a join or hallmark, make sure that these points of weakness are not directly opposite a split in the vertical mandrel as the stretching action is concentrated there. After each operation of the lever, the ring should be turned over to prevent it adopting the taper of the machine. Wide rings in particular can vary by a size from one edge to the other if not turned over.

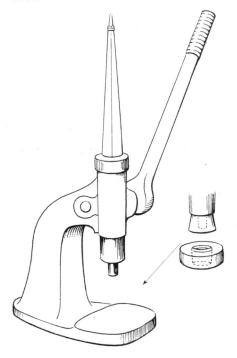

Fig. 1-27 Another form of ring-sizing machine, mainly for enlarging rings of uniform thickness such as most wedding rings. The vertical tapered arbor is split into four segments lengthwise and these are forced outwards when the lever is pulled down. A ring placed over the taper will therefore be stretched. At the bottom is a small press, that can be used with the parts shown inset to reduce the size of plain rings.

Rings of rectangular cross-section and wide rings with only a shallow curve will quickly lose their shapes as the stretching action is first on the edge of the ring. It is up to the jeweller to use his judgement in deciding what is and what is not acceptable because any complaints will eventually be placed at his door.

The majority of wedding rings at the time of writing seem to be of the 9ct gold machine-patterned (diamond-cut) variety. A 9ct ring with a join will invariably break at the join rather than stretch, but these modern ones are mostly made from seamless tube so, provided the pattern is not too deep in any one spot, they will stretch if they have been well annealed first. But keep an eye on the cuts of the pattern because these, like the hallmark, represent the weakest part of the ring.

These split mandrel machines are usually supplied with a set of thick discs with tapered holes in them which are used for reducing the size of plain rings. A disc is chosen that will just accommodate the ring and the two are placed under the press part of the machine as in the illustration inset in Fig. 1-27. The operation of the lever forces the ring into the taper, thus reducing its diameter. Their use is limited to narrow, plain rings for obvious reasons. On some machines, the taper in the discs is too slight. Consequently a ring forced into one of them becomes wedged so tightly that the force needed to free them marks or distorts them to a degree where the time saved by the machine in sizing is offset by the time needed to restore the ring to its original shape. So try it before you buy it.

Another snag I have found on the cheaper models is that deep and unnecessary size markings have been cut into the vertical taper which become transferred to the inside of rings made of soft metal. Also the vertical mandrel is perfectly circular when fully closed so that when fully opened it tends to create four flats on the

Fig. 1-28 A section of the tapered arbor of the machine in Fig. 1-27, shown closed and expanded with a ring round it. The better quality machines are perfectly round when fully expanded.

rings. This occurs only to a very minor degree on machines that are circular when fully opened. The exaggerated illustration (Fig. 1-28) will show what I mean.

The third machine called the Pinfold - which is the name of its maker, not one of its functions - is the predecessor of the last one and is shown in Fig. 1-29. Though it is much slower in operation, it achieves the same results and, as it forms the basis of a miniature screw press, can be adapted for other uses which I mention later in the book.

As shown in the inset of Fig. 1-29, the ring to be expanded is placed over a hole that is large enough to accept the tapered button but small enough to support the ring, the button is then forced through the ring by turning the hand wheel.

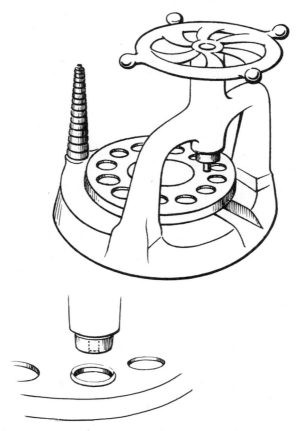

Fig. 1-29 A Pinfold machine, now obsolescent, which is slower than more recent machines but has many secondary uses as a miniature screw press.

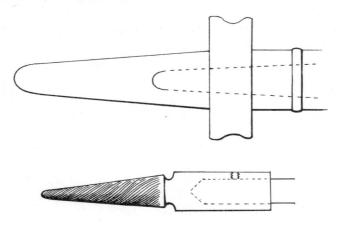

Fig. 1-30 (Top) With only one polishing spindle available, changing polishing mops can be a chore. An inside felt can be combined with an outside one on one spindle for polishing insides and outsides of the rings in the same operation.

Fig. 1-31(Above) A motor without tapered spindle can be fitted with an adaptor such as this, held by a grub screw. Left- and right-hand threads are available. Be sure the thread tends to screw the mop on, not off, when the mop is in use.

The reverse is achieved by putting the ring into one of the two tapered holes and forced down by a button of the appropriate size.

As many firms have updated themselves to the vertical taper machines it should be possible to pick up one of the Pinfold machines quite cheaply, though I did see one in an antique shop recently with a heavyprice tag on it.

Polishing Machine

The polishing machine described and illustrated in Fig. 1-2, is shown with a polishing mop on the left hand side. The mop is a 6 in (15 cm) diameter, 70 fold, Reflex finishing mop as made by Canning & Co specially for gold and silver finishing. The centre hole is capped on one side with a leather disc and by a tough fibre disc on the other, the leather disc should be nearest the motor. This mop is charged with Radio rouge when in use, which is a polishing compound also made by Cannings.

On the right hand spindle of the motor is a finger felt combined with an outside felt, with a tapered inner hole. These are also sold as separate items, but normally only one thing at a time can be fitted to a polishing taper so you would have to keep switching on and off in order to change from inside to outside felt, and so on. Also the bristle brush has only a small hole when purchased so it normally takes up the position on the taper used by the finger felts. To eliminate constant changing, I enlarge the hole in the brush so that it can be screwed to the thickest part of the taper, leaving the narrow end for the combined felt (Fig. 1-30) so that changing is only necessary when one or the other becomes worn out.

A motor made specifically for polishing usually comes with the polishing tapers ready fitted and a switch on the front so it only remains to fit the mop, felt and brush and switch on. The mop and felt will stay in position and the motor will be rotating in the right direction, that is: the front working half of the mop travelling downwards.

If you obtain a motor without tapers (Fig. 1-31) and have to order them you will need one left- and one right-hand, otherwise the screw on the taper may be in the wrong direction and throw the mop etc. off rather than screw them up tight. Be sure to specify the correct inside diameter to fit the motor spindle.

If your finances only run to a single-ended motor, it will be natural for a right-handed person to have the motor on the left and the spindle on the right so that a ring can be held in the right hand for polishing the inside on the tapered finger felt. If, when the motor is placed in this postion, its rotation is found to be in the wrong direction it can usually be reversed as follows. The normal terminal arrangement of an induction motor is shown in Fig. 1-32. The lead marked 2 should be fastened to terminal 4, and that marked 3 to terminal 1.

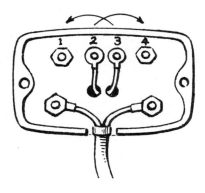

Fig. 1-32 A left-handed jeweller will probably find a single spindle polishing machine runs in the wrong direction. Altering wire 2 to terminal 4 and 3 to 1 will change the direction.

Chapter 2

Processes and Materials

Gilding and Silvering

Trade catalogues show gilding and silver plating outfits costing several hundreds of pounds, but for someone concerned only with repairing jewellery, the simplest of set-ups is sufficient. The most expensive item need only be the gold cyanide salts obtainable from some bullion dealers complete with instruction leaflet. The salts will be used mainly for restoring a gilt finish on an item that has been soldered.

Much new 9ct gold jewellery - trace chains in particular - are finished with an extremely thin coating of fine gold. It is so thin that just a touch on the polishing mop will remove it. The heat of soldering will burn it away and you are left with an unsightly discoloured patch which can only be eradicated by regilding. The simplest set-up for this is shown in Fig. 2-1.

Heating the Salts

The salts are mixed with water - some makers recommend distilled water, but I have never had any trouble using tap water - in proportions recommended by the manufacturer. Do not worry about measuring it too accurately; I have found it to be very tolerant stuff. It can only be kept in a vitreous enamel or glass container and because it has to be heated before use, this eliminates glass. A good quality domestic saucepan with a lid will suffice, provided the enamel on the inside is free from chips and blemishes. For heating I recommend the propane torch with the large jet, handheld. This way there is no possibility of being tempted to leave it to heat up while you do something else and allow it to boil over.

It will be quite hot enough when you can just bear your hand on the outside of the container. By then it should be just showing faint curls of steam. It will in fact work when it is only tepid, but the cooler it is, the darker the colour of the finish.

The anode should be made of stainless steel. A good quality knife blade will do. A piece of stainless steel or silver wire is needed to hang the article on. The anode is connected to the positive(+) terminal of a heavy duty 3 volt dry cell and the article to the negative (-) terminal. The articles to be gilt must be clean and free from grease.

It only remains to insert the anode and article in the solution for a few seconds without allowing them to touch. Then rinse them

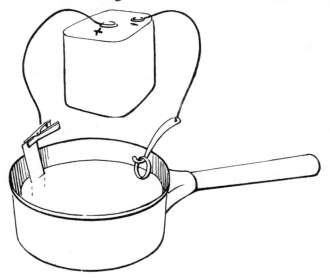

Fig. 2-1 After soldering new 9 carat jewellery the very thin pure gold gilding applied by the manufacturer can be restored in a simple set-up such as this using special plating salts.

both in running water and put the lid back on the container.

Sometimes, if the solution is too cool or becoming weak with age, the finish will be matt rather than bright, in which case a rub with the brass wire brush will brighten it.

Cyanide is a deadly poison but with care and commonsense, such as keeping it away from open cuts and the mouth and washing hands thoroughly after using it, it should be no more dangerous than the 250 volt electricity supply in the U.K. house.

For silvering, the set-up is the same except that the solution is silver cyanide and kept in a separate saucepan. Articles always come out of the silver solution with a matt finish but the brass wire brush will again brighten it. Silvering is used where intricate articles such as filigree cannot be restored to their original colour by the usual methods or where soldering has left a grey oxide colouring on a smooth surface and too much metal would have to be removed to eliminate it.

The 3 volt dry cell is the simplest power source, but a battery charger or car battery will work just as well, although if too high a voltage is employed discolouration will result.

Cleaning Articles

The rouge used in the polishing process is an oxide of iron ground to an extremely fine powder, which is mixed with grease and formed into bars. During polishing it becomes embedded in cavities and settings and leaves a thin film of grease over the polished article. This, along with any existing dirt, has to be removed.

The simplest way is to scrub the piece of jewellery in a bowl of hot water containing ammonia and some detergent. Bone-handled brushes are available for this job and last a long time, but an old tooth brush will do just as well. Traditionally the jewellery was dried, after cleaning, in a pot of heated boxwood dust which was purchased from jewellers' suppliers in miniature white sacks. It was kept in the inner pot of an old type cast iron glue pot, with water in the outer pot, which simmered continuously on the gas ring. It was effective but messy and tiny items, unless they had a wire attached to them, could be lost for some time in the sawdust.

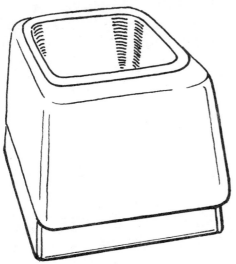

Fig. 2-2 An ultrasonic cleaning bath. It is partly filled with a cleaning fluid and operated from the mains electricity supply. A transducer in the base converts electrical energy into rapid shock waves through the fluid which has a fine scrubbing action on items placed in it.

That modern invention, the absorbent kitchen towel roll, does away with all that. If the jewellery is laid on a sheet of this paper, it dries quite quickly and one can see at a glance whether anything has been mislaid along the way.

The brush and detergent method will remove 90% of dirt and grease, but that last 10% wedged behind gemstones and dulling their ultimate brightness or stuck in the intricasies of filigree work, takes the edge off the final finish. An ultrasonic cleaning machine (Fig. 2-2) will remove all the dirt and leave you free to carry on with other work. These machines are extremely efficient but comparatively expensive. I can only say I would not be without one now.

Pendant Drill

The motor and part of the flexible shaft of a pendant drill can be seen at top right in the workbench illustration (Fig. 1-3); the remainder of it has been omitted for clarity. Although that master jeweller Benvenuto Cellini, might chuckle in his grave when I say it: I consider this a most essential piece of equipment. Even a cheap one with a fixed speed motor and a handpiece that needs a separate key to lock and unlock it, is better than none at all. A brace or an Archemides drill might be adequate for drilling holes, but the pendant drill can do an infinitely greater variety of work. The best system is one that has a variable speed motor controlled by a pedal like a sewing machine (Fig. 2-3) or one that has a finger button that will control the speed. One of these is shown in Fig. 2-4.

Used with various shaped dental burrs, a flexible drill takes a lot of awkward work out of stone setting such as enlarging settings and shaping them to fit stones of different shapes and sizes, work which otherwise would have to be done laboriously with gravers. Some

Fig 2.3 Pedal-operated speed control for a pendant drill.

shapes are shown in Fig. 2-5. Many is the time when a stone has to be supplied and the nearest one in stock is a fraction too large and the setting is such that it cannot be enlarged to take it. A diamond disc fitted in the pendant drill will quickly take a shaving from the stone and save you the trouble of parcelling up the ring and posting it off to the gem supplier and waiting a couple of weeks to get it back.

Fig. 2-4 Some jewellers prefer a finger-operated control for the pendant drill. It is near the drill itself.

There are various shaped Cratex wheels available. This is a mixture of emery and rubber which smoothly grinds away blemishes and engraving in awkward places. Small wire brushes can be fitted which will clean out cavities that would otherwise require a piece of wire wool on the end of a matchstick and much patience. A Cratex wheel and wire brush as well as a diamond disc are shown in Fig. 2-6.

For some reason unknown to me all these accessories come with a 2.3 mm diameter shank, as do a range of fine twist drills. These tend to break rather easily, making it an expensive way of drilling holes. There are alternatives available. Your dentist uses little sterile packs of rivets for repairing teeth. They are supplied with one rivet and matching drill in a pack. The drill is used once then discarded. Need I say more? Get to know your dentist.

Fig. 2-5 Three common and useful shapes of burrs for use in a pendant drill. Metal can be shaped or textured with them. Many other shapes and various sizes are available.

The other alternative is a pair of punch pliers. Though I have never found any suitable ready-made ones on the market, they are quite simple to construct from a pair of flat- or snipe-nosed pliers. The jaws are softened and a hole is drilled through them with a 1mm drill as shown in Fig. 2-7. The smooth shank of the drill is then cut off and fitted into one of the jaws by either rivetting or a clamp screw, leaving about 2 mm protruding. There is no need to re-harden the jaws as even in the annealed state, the metal is harder than most of the sheet material a jeweller uses.

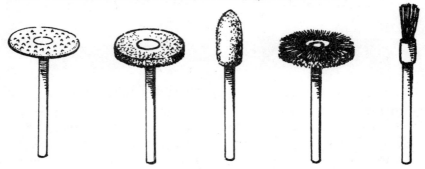

Fig. 2-6 As well as drills and burrs for the pendant drill, there are diamond grinding wheels, Cratex wheels (a mixture of emery powder and rubber) of various shapes, brushes and polishing felts.

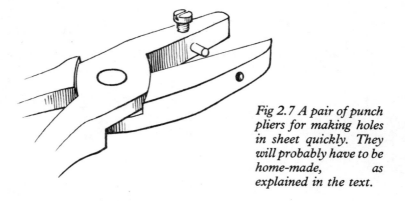

Fig 2.7 A pair of punch pliers for making holes in sheet quickly. They will probably have to be home-made, as explained in the text.

Gold and Silver Materials

The amount and form of gold and other precious metals a jobbing jeweller carries in stock will depend on the quantity of work and the size of his purse and what can be obtained by way of scrap. Below is a selection that will cover most needs.

9ct yellow gold round wire: 0.60 in, 0.40 in and 0.20 in diameter

9ct yellow gold D-shaped wire: 0.60 in by 0.90 in and 0.60 in by 0.150 in

9ct yellow gold sheet: 0.012in. thick and 0.035 in thick

18ct yellow D-shape 0.060in by 0.090 in

18ct white D-shape 0.060 in by 0.090 in

Platinum D-shape 0.060 in by 0.090 in

The two sizes of D-shape wire will provide shanks and sizing pieces for most gem rings and signets. Intermediate sizes would save a lot of waste and filing but would require a greater outlay. Nine carat white gold is not very common except in the settings of cheap eternity rings, so just a little could be purchased as the need arises.

In the general run of repairs, 18ct yellow gold will be needed only for ring shanks and these will be mainly ladies gem rings so the one size will cover most work. The next most common demand for 18ct yellow is to build up the base of settings of the same type of ring, but if the base of the setting is worn, the ring usually needs a new shank as well, so the old shank can be used to build up the base of the setting. The same applies to 18ct white gold and platinum.

The yellow gold alloys are of a standard colour and the only specification needed when ordering is to state whether soft or half-hard is required. As it is easier to soften a half-hard piece than vice versa it is best to order the latter.

A large range of 18ct white golds is available of varying whiteness and toughness. The nickel alloys are not so white as the platinum/palladium alloy. Also the nickel alloy oxidizes whereas the platinum/palladium alloy does not.

This fact is one way of distinguishing white gold nickel alloys from platinum itself, which is a necessary piece of information if the shank is not stamped. A guide to distinguishing platinum/palladium white gold from platinum is that the white gold alloy will polish brilliantly and easily on a rouge mop whereas platinum will hardly be touched.

A range of silver material similar to the 9ct gold will also be needed.

Sometimes a 22ct wedding ring turns up that needs enlarging so much that stretching would make it too thin, in which case a piece of 22ct gold will need to be added. Any old 22ct rings that come your way should be kept for this purpose as holding them in reserve will turn out to be much cheaper than ordering new gold from a dealer for occasional jobs.

Appropriate solders are available for each of these metals and are usually classified by melting point as: 'easy', 'medium' and 'hard'. For the majority of work, the easy grade is best as there is less chance of melting other soldered joins on the piece and having it collapse, but occasionally a panel of hard will be needed where subsequent soldering might open the first joint.

Borax is the flux used for all these solders. It can be bought as a white powder and mixed with water into a paste for ease of use. It is also available as a hard cone, which has to be rubbed on a wet slate to produce a paste. Auflux, a commercial product, I find the most convenient flux for repairs. It is a thin yellow liquid which has less tendency to boil and blow off the piece of solder when heated. It also has a slight deoxidizing action which is a help when an item has to be reheated several times.

Gemstone Stocks

It would not be practical for the jobbing jeweller to keep a stock of gemstones sufficient to cope with every job that comes along, but as the most popular stones at any one time are of necessity at the cheaper end of the gemstone range, it is possible to stock enough to cater for about half the empty settings that come his way.

For several years now it has been well worth stocking garnets between 0.5 mm and 3 mm in half millimetre steps, as well as half pearls for 0.5 mm to 2 mm and dark sapphires from 0.5 mm to 2.5mm.

White and coloured paste stones, marcasites and white synthetic spinels are available in boxes of twelve graduated sizes. They are reasonably cheap and very handy to have by you.

Reconstructed turquoise, which is powdered turquoise reformed into cabochons, is slightly paler and softer than natural turquoise but the 'cabs' are very cheap and easier to set than the natural stone because of their uniformity.

Occasionally a setting will come along that is such an unusual shape or size that it will be nearly impossible to get a ready-made stone to fit. For such jobs it is handy to have a piece of mother-of-pearl or paua shell which can be sawn or filed with existing bench tools to fit the setting.

For the remainder, you will have to find a gem merchant specializing in one-off jobs. You can expect to pay up to ten times more for the stones because of the handling time involved. Their prices and services vary enormously, so it is best to shop around.

Jewellers' Findings

The quaint name 'jewellers' findings' is applied to all the ready-made bits and pieces a jeweller uses in the repair and manufacture of jewellery. A glance in any supplier's catalogue will show the vast range available (see Fig. 2-8). Some of them, such as revolver safety catches for brooches and bolt ring catches for necklets and bracelets, cannot be made by hand and will have to be bought, but it is a great advantage to be able to make as much as you can yourself. For instance, it is not too expensive to buy a large assortment of brooch pins but when it comes to matching one to a brooch you have to find near enough the right diameter tube, matching the metal colour and use the right thickness and length of pin.

Often you end up with everything right except the length of pin. You fit it to the brooch, snip it off to length and file a new point, only to discover the pin was gilt on nickel or silver plate on brass, so when you have polished the new point half the pin is the wrong colour. Often the time spent sorting through a large assortment of pins would be better spent soldering a piece of tube to a piece of wire. Tube is fairly easy to make and draw down, as is explained in the next chapter. Nickel and brass wire is also easy to obtain and draw down and you will know exactly what you are getting.

Hollow gold and silver beads of 2.5 mm and 3 mm diameter are a useful item to have in stock as they can be used for decoration and terminal pieces and also enable you to make your own ear-fittings, which can be a big saving. Although it is simple enough to solder a bead on the end of a wire and bend it into the hook shape of an ear-wire using the round-nosed pliers, it is not so easy to make a matching pair or several identical ones that way.

Using the simple jig illustrated in Fig. 2-9, it is possible to bend up any number of identical ear-wires with either ball or loop ends. It consists of a 4 in (10 cm) length of ¾ in (20 mm) wooden dowel with a piece of ¼ in (6 mm) and 1/16 in (1.5 mm) steel rod (sections of nails are ideal) embedded in the end. A 1¼ in (30 mm) length of gold or silver wire between 0.025 in to 0.027 in (0.63 mm to 0.68

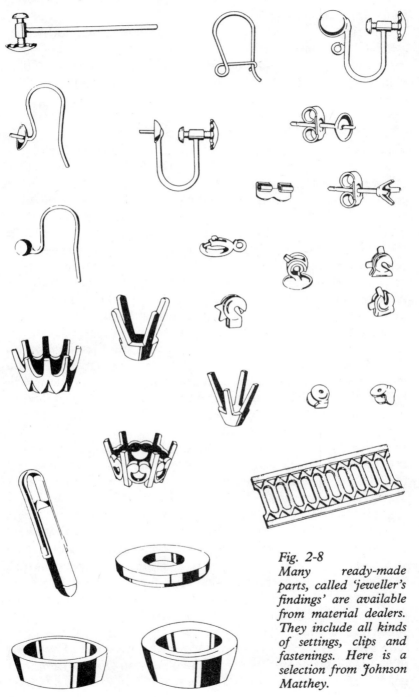

Fig. 2-8
Many ready-made parts, called 'jeweller's findings' are available from material dealers. They include all kinds of settings, clips and fastenings. Here is a selection from Johnson Matthey.

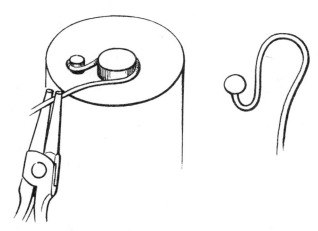

Fig. 2-9 A simple jig for making ear wires for earrings, with either bell or loop ends.

mm) thick has the end bent into a loop to fit over the small rod, the tail is then gripped about ⅛ in (3 mm) from the end in the round nosed pliers and curled round the larger rod. For bead-ended wires, the process is the same except that the bead is soldered on to the wire first and a loop formed beneath it to fit the small rod.

A similar arrangement can be used to make safety wires with the addition of a piece of tube let into the dowel in the position as shown in Fig. 2-10. The inside diameter of the tube should be sufficient to take the thickness of the earwire. The end ⅛ in (3 mm) of a 1½ in. (38 mm) length of wire is bent at right angles and the short end fitted into the tube. The remainder is then wound completely round the small rod and over the top of the large rod and brought into line with the tube. It is then eased off the rods and the short end that was in the tube formed into a hook as shown.

The same system of employing dowel and short lengths of rod can be used to make a jig for forming the small safety pins used on brooch safety chains. The end of the wire about 0.02 in thick is fitted in the tube then bent level with the surface of the dowel. It is taken twice around the first pin, once round the two others as shown in Fig. 2-11 then snipped off leaving sufficient for the pin. The piece that was in the tube is formed into a hook to take the end of the pin.

Other items very useful in making your own findings are round flat discs of various sizes, which as far as I know, are not obtainable

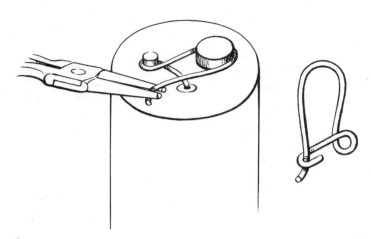

Fig. 2-10 A similar jig to that in Fig. 2-9, but for making safey wires.

ready-made. The usual tools for making them are cap punches, which can be obtained in sets from tool suppliers (Fig. 2-12). In use, the piece of material from which the disc is to be made is placed on a soft steel or brass block. (A hard steel block will quickly take the edge off the punch). The punch is placed upright in the desired spot and given an initial blow with the hammer to mark out the disc, the punch is then tilted slightly and hit again, tilted at the opposite angle and hit again and so on until the disc parts company with the surrounding metal. It is a laborious method and considering the number of discs one needs for pearl cups and assisted joints, etc, it is worth while making the following accessory shown in Fig. 2-13, for the Pinfold ring sizing machine.

If you have access to a small lathe, it is a very simple job to turn up the punch 'A' from a piece of ½ in (12 mm) diameter silver steel

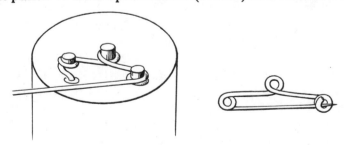

Fig. 2-11 Still another jig for making your own findings, in this case a safety pin (shown inset) for a brooch safety chain.

rod. Drill and tap the clamp screw hole and harden and temper it. The hole should be a snug fit on the stem of the machine where the brass buttons usually go (normally this is 5/16 in diameter). A ⅛ in Whitworth thread or a suitable metric one, will suffice for the clamp screw. The most useful size of cap would be about 3/16 in (5 mm) diameter, so the business end of the punch 'C' should be turned down to that diameter. It is best to drill the hole in the die 'B' first and turn down the punch to fit, because twist drills, unless they are in perfect condition, tend to drill slightly oversize.

If you have no lathe to use, you could use a piece of 1 in (25 mm) long ½ in (12 mm) diameter mild steel rod for the body of the punch. After making the hole to fit the Pinfold machine at the top end, drill the opposite end with a 3/16 in (4.75 mm) drill and use the top ½ in (12 mm) of the drill shank for the actual punch as was done with the punch pliers earlier, using a second clamp screw to hold it in place.

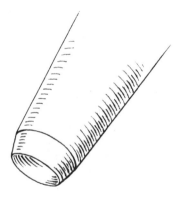

Fig. 2-12 A cap punch as supplied by a material dealer.

The die 'B' can be made from an old flat file 3/16 in (say 5 mm) to ¼ in (6mm) thick. If heated to bright red, held at that temperature for a short while, then allowed to cool slowly, it should be soft enough to cut with a hacksaw and drill. A 2 in (50 mm) length of it should be sufficient to span the gap in the bed of the Pinfold and leave enough each side for clamping down.

When the roughness has been removed from one side of the piece of file and the 3/16 in (4.75 mm) hole drilled, the last two-thirds of the hole should be made wider by drilling from the opposite side with a larger diameter drill, otherwise the discs will pile up in the hole and be difficult to remove.

To reharden the die, heat it to a bright carrot red (not cherry as is so often given in the instructions. Most cherries I have seen are dark red and tool steel will not harden if quenched from that colour). Then plunge it into a bucket of tepid water. It will now be hard but very brittle. After checking with a file that it is really hard, clean the smooth side with a piece of emery paper and warm it gently with the propane torch until the surface turns yellow to straw colour, then quench it again. This will temper it and remove the brittleness.

There are two bolts holding the brass circle in position on the base of the Pinfold machine. If these are removed the circle taken off and two pieces of mild steel bar drilled to take the bolts as shown in Fig. 2-13 the die can be clamped in position. With the punch in position, the hole in the die lined up with it, and a piece of metal placed over the hole, it is only a matter of lowering and raising the punch to stamp out as many discs as are required. Larger

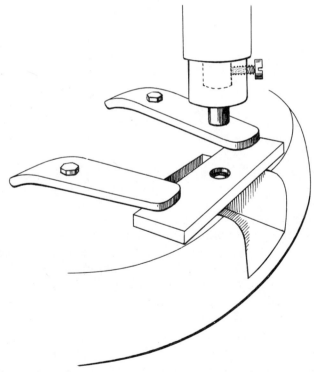

Fig. 2-13 An accessory for producing discs at a reasonable rate, using a Pinfold machine (fig 1.29) or similar miniature screw press. The parts to be made are the punch with its socket A, the die B, and the two straps to hold the die in position under the punch.

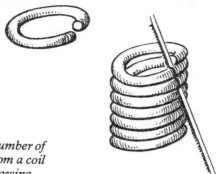

Fig. 2-14 Making a number of
jump rings quickly from a coil
of softened wire by sawing.

and smaller sets of punches and dies can be made in the same manner but the larger the disc needed, the thinner the metal it is made of, to avoid overstressing the machine.

Making Jump Rings

Jump rings - small rings for fastenings - must be the most common finding used by a jeweller and the easiest to make. It is merely a matter of wrapping a piece of wire of the desired thickness round a piece of rod of the appropriate diameter. The rod around which the wire is wrapped is usually called a spit. Cardboard tubes of nickel wire in assorted diameters available from tool suppliers are ideal for making jump rings.

The wire (softened) is clamped against the spit in a pair of pliers and wound around the spit spiral fashion, taking care to keep the turns tightly together. When released from the pliers, the coil springs open slightly, making it easy to remove from the spit. When the coil is sawn down vertically as shown in Fig. 2-14 the result is a quantity of ready to use jump rings.

For oval rings the process is slightly different. One uses an oval spit (oval nails or slightly flattened round rod) but the tendency for the coil to unwind slightly when released would result in the coil being firmly clamped to the oval spit as the oval shape prevents it unwinding. To overcome this, the spit is first wrapped in three or four thicknesses of tissue paper then, when the coil is completed, the whole is held in the torch flame until the tissue is burnt away, the coil softened, and the tension released. It can then easily be removed from the spit.

To make a large quantity of identical rings - to refurbish the

Lord Mayor's chain of office for instance - fit the spit into the chuck of a handbrace and clamp the brace in the bench vice. Bend the first ½ in (12 mm) of the ring wire at right angles and slide it between two jaws of the chuck. Wind the handle of the brace with the left hand and guide the wire on to the spit with the right and the job will be done in a matter of seconds. See Fig. 2-15.

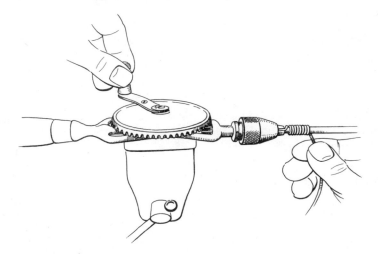

Fig. 2-15 A quick way of coiling wire when a large number of jump rings is needed for, say, a medallion chain.

The saw breaking task of cutting down a long coil can be avoided if the following gadget is used. Tool suppliers usually stock a small device resembling a pair of pliers which enable retailers to cut bloodlessly through rings which customers cannot remove from their fingers. It utilizes a small circular saw for this purpose and spare blades are available. One of these spare blades is fitted to the spindle of a small induction motor as shown in Fig. 2-16.

A block of steel with a hole just large enough to take the coil of jump rings has a slot cut through from one side into the hole to allow the saw blade to rotate and cut into the coil. The blade is lubricated with candle or beeswax and the coil fed down into the hole and a splatter of jump rings emerges from the bottom. To keep friction to a minimum, the blade should be set so it just penetrates the coil and no more.

Though it is not usually economical to make your own earscrews, the occasion sometimes arises where an unusual one

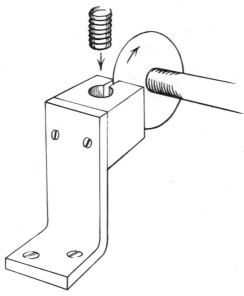

Fig. 2-16 A quick way of cutting a coiled wire when making jump rings, using a slitting saw with an easily-made jig.

has to be matched up or an urgent job comes along just when you have run out of screws. All that is needed to cope with these situations is a 1/16 in Standard Whitworth tap and die or a suitable metric set to make the working parts of the screw.

As there are three soldered joints in close proximity the large disc used for turning the screw should be soldered on with high melting point (hard) solder and so should the tube. Then when the two are screwed together, the domed disc can be soldered on with easy solder without fear of the other joints melting. If there is any chance of the solder running down the screw and making it solid, a

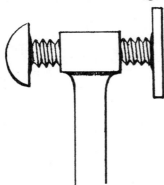

Fig. 2-17 In emergency, it may be necessary to make an earscrew like this. The text explains how to solder the three joints without fear of one melting.

47

spot of rouge powder made into paste with water and painted on the thread will prevent this happening (Fig. 2-17).

Items hardly worth keeping in stock because there is so little call for them are ear clips. On the odd occasion when one is needed, it is a simple job to bend one up from round wire as shown in Fig. 2-18.

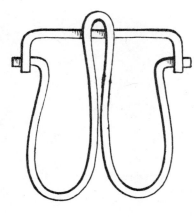

Fig. 2-18 Ear clips when needed can be made quite simply from wire.

Chapter 3

Basic Techniques

Melting and Casting Scrap

The biggest advantages of having a set of rolls is that one can re-use all the bits and pieces of gold and silver that accummulate over the weeks and which are too small or misshapen to be of any further use. Also one tends to accummulate a surplus of sizing pieces: the small segments cut from rings when reducing their size. If these are kept in separate boxes according to their carat along with any worn-out shanks of known carat these can be melted down and re-used.

Avoid using scrap that has a lot of soldered joints such as old expanding watch bracelets or trace chain. It can be used, but not too much in any one melt otherwise the excessive amount of solder will tend to lower the melting point of the resulting metal and if you need to use hard solder on it you might find the metal melting before the solder.

Thoroughly examine the scrap before consigning it to the melting pot, looking for silver solder repairs on gold items and particularly lead solder repairs on watch cases. The square or octagonal fronts of old wrist watches wear at the corners first and are often filled with lead solder and painted over with gold paint by crafty watchmakers whose sole aim is to keep dust away from their beloved movements. The slightest trace of lead in a melt will ruin it; the resulting ingot will be brittle and crack easily when stressed. Remove all rivets from hinges and, if they are corroded in, cut out the whole hinge and consign it to the lemel pot rather than risk using it. A lemel pot can be a coffee jar containing bench sweepings and bits of metal of unknown quality, turned into cash annually to take the sting out of the income tax bill.

For the small amount of scrap a repairer uses, the crucible

49

known as 'square fletcher' is the handiest and the 50mm square size adequate. They come without a handle but none of the catalogues I have seen lists one, so I have always had to make my own. The illustration Fig. 3-1 shows how this is done. The material is ½ in by 1/16 in mild steel strip and the handle is a piece of 1 in (25 mm) dowel slotted lengthways with a saw and held in place with a nut and bolt. The steel strip is filed half-way through at the bends with a three cornered or square file to make them sharper and easier to bend. Usually, if the handle is about 9 in (23 cm) long, in the short time it takes to melt the 30-odd grams of metal the heat does not have time to travel right up the handle but the piece of dowel removes the element of chance and saves you the job of picking up hundreds of small balls of metal with eyeglass and tweezers from the bench. They are like spilt mercury - not many balls stay on the bench!

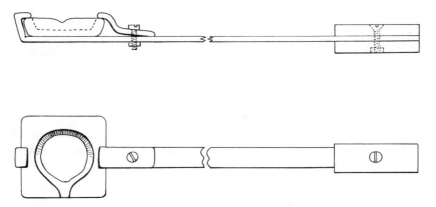

Fig 3.1 A small crucible, known as a 'square fletcher', for melting small amounts of precious metal scrap. How to make one is explained in the text.

Use a separate crucible for different metals as there are always traces left behind in the flux. Silver will lower the quality of 9ct gold, and 9ct gold will lower the quality of 18ct, and should you need to send anything to the assay office to be hallmarked and it is below quality it will be broken up and sent back in pieces. For this reason I always put half a gram of 18ct in with a 30 gram 9ct melt, just in case.

The figure of 30 grams is the amount a 50mm square fletcher will take comfortably and also the amount needed to fill a 3 in (75 mm) long ¼ in square ingot mould, and a ¼ in square ingot will fit comfortably into the largest groove on most hand-operated rolls.

It has been my experience that ready-made ¼ in square vertical ingot moulds are not easily come by and in case you have the same difficulty the Fig. 3-2 No.2 will show two ways to overcome this problem. The square mould is made from two 3 in lengths of 1 in by ¼ in mild steel bar and two 3 in lengths of ¼ inch square bar screwed or tack welded together as shown and one half attached by either method to the base plate which is made from any reasonably heavy flat piece of steel. A funnel is filed into the top as shown to make it easier to pour into. A flat ingot mould to produce an ingot ⅛ in by 1 in for rolling into sheet can be made in the same way using the appropriate sections of steel. It will be obvious that by increasing the overlap of the two halves the ingot can be made narrower than an inch.

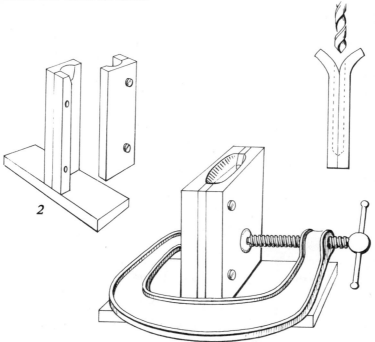

Fig 3.2 *Making a square mould for producing ¼ inch or other small sizes of ingot.*

The second mould is made from two 4 in (10 cm) lengths of ¼ in by ¼ in bar, bent apart at the top as shown. They are gripped tightly in the vice and drilled almost to the bottom with a ¼ in drill. Both moulds when in use can be held together with an ordinary G-clamp.

The inside surfaces of the moulds should be made as smooth as possible to facilitate the easy removal of the ingot and should be blackened with the torch to prevent the liquid metal adhering to them. A light film of oil on the inside surfaces also helps in this way.

As there is always the chance of a slight spillage, the mould should be placed in a metal tray of some description. The lid of a large biscuit tin fits the bill nicely and if your finances do not run to a proper brazing hearth for the melting process, the tin itself, fitted out with fire bricks, can take its place.

With the scrap weighed and placed in the crucible and the crucible nestling in the fire bricks, sprinkle a little borax powder over the scrap then apply the propane torch, using the largest jet. A final word of warning - make sure before you heat the scrap that it does not contain any sealed hollow pieces such as hollow gold charms or old-fashioned torpedo type cuff-link ends. If there are any, pierce them thoroughly otherwise the air contained in them expands with the heat until they explode.

When the scrap is well on the way to melting, remove the crucible from the fire bricks and, still keeping the torch on it, rest the crucible at the base of the ingot mould so that part of the flame envelopes it. Keep it there until the mould is far too hot to touch but not so hot that it glows. Then return the crucible to the fire bricks. It is impossible to pour molten metal into a cold mould; it just freezes on impact and you end up with a misshapen blob stuck on the top.

When the metal looks fluid enough to pour, keep the flame on it for at least another minute to give it heat to spare because the mould is still colder than the metal and will take some of the heat from it. A short or incompletely formed ingot is usually the result of the mould or the metal or both insufficiently heated.

When the metal is ready to pour, keep the flame on it all the time, rest the edge of the crucible on the lip of the mould and pour it in a continuous, unbroken stream. Any breaks will invariably leave you with a faulty ingot.

After the ingot has cooled and has been removed, the next step is to pickle it to remove any flux that might have adhered to it. Sometimes a pocket of flux is formed in the surface which the acid will not remove, in which case gouge it out with a scriber. Hard flux is almost like glass and although it may not damage the surface of the rolls, it may stick to them and leave an indentation on any metal rolled afterwards.

To roll down a square or round ingot, close the rolls fully and poke the ingot into the grooves until you reach one that it will not enter. Slacken off the rolls until they will accept it, then tighten them down half a turn and roll the ingot through the groove. Hold it as it emerges from the other side and, when it is free, rotate it through 90 degrees and take it back through the same groove. If you don't rotate it at each pass, you will end up with two flanges running the length of the ingot.

If it becomes hard to roll or the ends of the resulting square wire show signs of splitting, it is time to anneal the wire and cut off the split end, if there is one.

With a flat ingot to be turned into sheet, it is just a matter of placing the ingot in the smooth section of the rolls, clamping them down and rolling. It is even more important when rolling sheet to make sure that the rolls and the sheet are completely clean. Even a dust mote will leave its trace on the metal and any mark will have to be removed at some later stage.

Always keep the surface of the rolls slightly oiled and parted when not in use. If the rolls are slightly inaccurate, you may find the strip of sheet developing a lateral curve, in which case turn it over each time it is passed through. If it is very pronounced, you may have to alter the setting by advancing or retarding the gear controlling the nearest bearing by one tooth.

Wire Drawing

When the wire has been rolled down small enough to fit the largest hole in the draw plate, it has to be annealed. Using the large jet on the propane torch with a bushy flame so as not to overheat or melt the wire, heat it to medium red and work your way from one end to the other and then back again to eliminate any hard spots. When it is cool, file a slender point at one end sufficient to allow it to pass through the hole in the draw plate and leaving enough to be gripped with the tongs. Apply a blob of oil to the back of the hole, then grip the end in the tongs and pull. Keep the direction of pull in line with the hole otherwise it will coil up when released and be difficult to straighten out again. Also keep one foot braced behind you all the time in case the wire breaks (See Figs. 3-3 and 3-4).

When the end of the wire is about to pass through the hole, hold the tongs in one hand if possible while gripping the wire near the draw plate with the other because the wire has the tendency to flick over when it is released from the hole and if you happen to be in the line of fire it can give you a nasty dig. If the wire is too long or too hard to pull with one hand, turn your head away. One-eyed jewellers have a hard time making a living.

Fig 3.3 (Left) The wrong way to draw wire through a draw plate if you do not have a draw bench. The cushion will certainly be necessary when the wire snaps!
Fig 3.4 (Right) When drawing wire, keep your balance by having one foot behind you. The wire coming through the draw hole should be at right angles to the plate. Here the plate leans slightly forwards and the wire is still kept square to it.

When the wire becomes hard and difficult to draw, anneal it again. This saves energy and wear on the draw plate.

Bullion dealers supply seamless tube in various materials and in a range of diameters and wall thicknesses and this can be drawn down in the draw plate in the same way as wire. However the need often arises where the inside diameter is right for the job but the outside is not, but when it is pulled through the draw plate both diameters are reduced. To prevent the inside diameter being reduced, use a length of oiled piano wire (springy steel wire obtainable from watch material and model engineers suppliers), which is a sliding fit in the tube. Slide it to the end and carry out drawing as normal. As the tube is drawn, it becomes harder and springier and so, as it emerges from the hole in the draw plate it tends to enlarge again by a minute fraction, just sufficient to allow the piano wire to be withdrawn with ease.

It is not practical to make your own seamless tube, but tube with a seam in it is quite easy to make and has many uses such as for the pin joints mentioned earlier.

A strip of sheet metal is first formed into a U-shape lengthways by placing it over a semi-circular groove filed into a block of brass or mild steel and forced into it by tapping a rod of the right diameter down on to it as shown in Fig. 3-5. One end is then bent over roughly into tube form and a point formed on it to allow it to pass through the hole, which shapes the remainder into a neat tube. In theory it should be possible to calculate the width of strip necessary to give a certain diameter of tube but in practice it is mainly a case of trial and error.

If you need tube larger than the largest hole in the draw plate, a makeshift plate of brass or steel with one or two holes drilled through it and tapered on one side will work, but only for tube.

Soldering Techniques

Soldering is the process of joining two pieces of metal together with a third piece of lower melting point. When the third piece (solder) is a lead alloy, the process is known as 'soft soldering'. Tin is the metal alloyed with the lead and by varying the proportions, the melting point ranges between 150 to 200 degrees C.

When working with precious metals the solder has to be near enough the same quality or purity and colour as the parent metals,

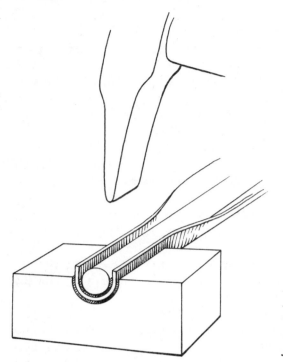

Fig 3.5 How to form seamed tube, using a rod and a strip of the tube metal in a groove filed in a metal block.

so of necessity the melting points of the solder are high by comparison. The melting point of 9ct yellow gold is around 900 degrees C, 9ct easy solder melts at about 700 degrees C and 9ct hard solder at about 770 degrees C. 18ct yellow gold melts at just over 900 degrees C, 18ct easy solder at around 740 degrees C, and hard at around 860 degrees C. The figures for sterling silver are similar to those for 9ct yellow. It is not possible to be precise about these figures as they vary from manufacturer to manufacturer and as I mentioned earlier, your own 9ct ingot will have a lower than 900 degrees C melting point if too much solder is included in the scrap.

All these solders come under the general heading of hard solder so do not be misled into thinking that only the high melting point solder is to be used when hard soldering is mentioned.

The principle made use of in soldering is that of capillary action, which means that the solder has a strong inclination to flow into clean narrow cracks; the cleaner and narrower, the stronger the inclination. Two pieces of wire are filed square at the ends which are placed together and the general area covered with flux to prevent them oxidizing when heated. If a piece of solder is placed over the point of contact and the whole of it heated evenly until the solder melts, instead of rolling up into a little ball and staying put, the solder will be drawn into the crack and join the two pieces of wire together.

The important word in the last sentence was 'evenly', and it is the uneven heating of the metals that causes the learner solderer the most heartache. It takes time and practice to bring the two halves of a proposed joint to the right temperature simultaneously. The result of not doing so is that the solder pauses in an undecided ball for a second then nips down whichever side gets hot enough first and ignores the join completely.

It is difficult enough when the pieces to be joined are of equal section and volume. When they are not - for example when soldering a small loop on to a large silver disc or coin - the problem is far worse. Unless great care is taken, the loop will reach its melting point before the disc is even discoloured.

A good practice piece for the beginner to work on is making a bracelet length of silver oval linked chain. As he will have a usable item if the exercise is successful, there is a stronger inclination to get it right. Silver being a better conductor of heat than gold is more trying: it heats up and cools down faster making it more difficult to heat the joins evenly. After that, working one of the more expensive and less temperamental materials will be relatively easy.

Using Lap Joints

Hard solder used in jewellery work is strong enough in most cases to allow ordinary butt joints (Fig. 3-6) to be used, that is, just placing two pieces squarely together and soldering them. In cases where the join will be subjected to bending action, such as the thin

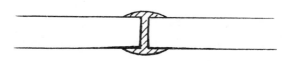

Fig 3.6 A simple butt joint, which is used for some repairs, but not when the metal is likely to be bent or is thin.

shank of a man's signet ring where anything gripped in the hand presses against the shank, or thin wire bangles which are distorted each time they are forced over the broad part of the hand, a lap joint is used (Fig. 3-7). The two faces of the join are filed to a matching angle to give a much larger area of contact and thus making a stronger join. Very thin wires, such as ear-wires and brooch pins, are joined in this way.

Fig 3.7 A lap joint like this is stronger than a butt joint and is used for thin wires and for extra strength.

When soldering two large flat surfaces together such as building up the head of a signet ring by soldering a piece of sheet on to it, the two pieces of metal will have to be held together under light pressure, such as by gripping with the tweezers, otherwise the sheet will rise up and float on the solder, leaving a gap around the edge that cannot be filled (Fig. 3-8). When making this kind of join it is best to melt the solder on to the heaviest piece first then apply the fluxed thinner piece and re-melt the solder. If, after melting the solder on to the heavier part, there is the slightest signs of oxidization or the solder appears to have avoided a particular spot, pickle it and clean it with the brass wire brush and reflux it before proceeding further.

Fig 3.8 If a small piece with a relatively large surface is being soldered to another such surface, the solder will push them apart as shown unless they are held together by light pressure.

In the case of two pieces to be soldered of considerably different volume, like the disc and loop mentioned earlier, the solder should be melted onto the larger volume piece first and the smaller piece applied afterwards.

One very common use of solder in jewellery repairs is for building up worn parts. Small rings in particular, if used for suspending heavy objects such as large St. Christopher medals or gold coins, tend to become worn in one spot only as shown in Fig. 3-9. These spots can be rebuilt by melting a piece of solder into them after first cleaning with a needle file and fluxing.

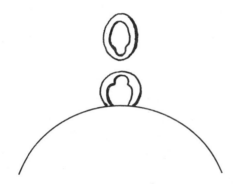

Fig 3.9 Solder is commonly used for building up worn parts such as these rings holding a pendant.

The commonest cause of a faulty soldered join is dirt or grease. If the surfaces are not perfectly clean and thoroughly fluxed the solder will not flow properly. The next most common cause is overheating of the join. If the solder does not flow easily after reaching its melting point, additional heat will only destroy the alloy of the solder and even if you do persuade it to flow, you will have a brittle joint. If things do not go right the first time, pickle and clean the piece and start again using a fresh piece of solder.

The solder purchased from bullion dealers usually comes in small panels 1½ inch by ¾ in by 0.010 in thick and in use is cut into small squares or rectangles by first cutting, comb fashion, into the narrow end with the tin snips then crossways with the fingers pressed against the fragments as shown in Fig. 3-10 to prevent them scattering as they are cut. On the workbench in Fig. 1-3 to the left of the peg can be seen a rectangular object with three U-shapes on its surface. This is a porcelain slab with three indentations in its surface. They are purchased from artists' suppliers and are intended for the mixing of water colour paints, but they form excellent receptacles for bits of solder, silver at one end and 9ct easy solder at the other.

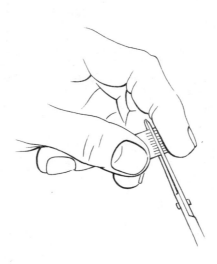

Fig 3.10 Solder is usually bought in small panels and should be cut for use into tiny squares (paillons) by cutting comb fashion and then across as shown. The first and second fingers hold the panel and the first finger steadies the end being cut with snips to prevent the tiny pieces from scattering. The paillons would normally be cut smaller than shown here for jewellery work.

Filing Action

Most people, I should imagine, are familiar with the use and action of a file. The only specialist application in jewellery work is when filing the circular, convex outer surface of a ring. To avoid ending up with a series of flat sections or facets, both the ring and the file must be kept in continuous motion. The ring, held in the left hand and supported against the peg, should be rotated against the cut of the file so that the file travels round the circumference of the ring for the length of one stroke. At the same time, the file should be rotated anti-clockwise as it is moved forward so it starts its cut on one side of the ring and follows the convex surface of the ring ending up on the other side of the ring at the end of the stroke. Figs. 3-11 and 3-12 will perhaps explain the action better.

There is always a tendency when tidying up a soldered join in a ring to concentrate on the join. This is all very well while removing the excess solder with a few short strokes, but if continued too far, the ring will be thinner at the join than elsewhere. It is better to

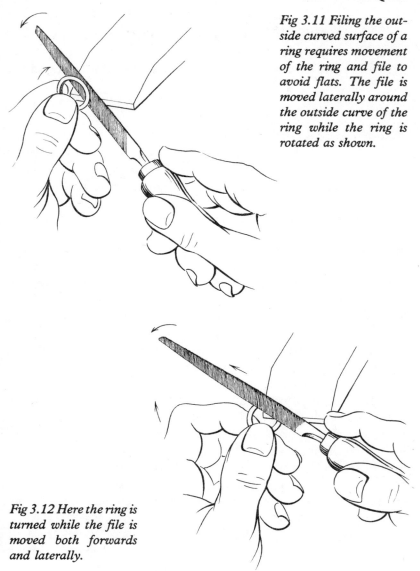

*Fig 3.11 Filing the out-
side curved surface of a
ring requires movement
of the ring and file to
avoid flats. The file is
moved laterally around
the outside curve of the
ring while the ring is
rotated as shown.*

*Fig 3.12 Here the ring is
turned while the file is
moved both forwards
and laterally.*

have the ring a shade thinner all over than have a flat spot pin-
pointing where the work was carried out.

One is often requested to remove the engraving from the heads
of signet rings and this is done with the file. The thing to watch
here is that when filing flat surfaces the teeth of the file tend to clog
easily so that just when you think the job is finished, the next

stroke puts a few more lines across it. The secret is not to press too hard and as soon as a deeper line appears on the filed surface turn the file over and poke out the clogged teeth with either the point of the scriber or a file card, which is a steel wire brush with very short stiff bristles.

The Piercing Saw

Though the piercing saw is made for cutting intricate designs in sheet material, in jewellery repair work it is used for all cutting work that requires a saw because the blade is so fine that the minimum of precious metal is turned into 'sawdust'.

The blade is fitted into the frame with the teeth pointing down towards the handle so that it cuts on the downstroke. After one end of the blade is clamped in the frame and the other end is resting in the opposite clamp, the frame is compressed slightly by pressing against the edge of the bench. Enter the other end of the blade in the other clamp and tighten it. When the frame is released the blade is taut and pings like a guitar string when plucked.

New blades tend to jam a little and a light rubbing of beeswax or candle wax will ease its passage. Items being sawn should always be firmly supported against the bench peg as well as being held in the hand. Most blade breakages occur when the article moves a little when half way through a stroke. It is not possible to hold something rigid enough in the fingers alone to prevent this. Another point when blades break is on the final stroke when the thickness of the last bit of metal is such that it fits between two teeth and causes a sudden jam. It is best if possible to break that final bit with the fingers. This also happens when cutting thin sheet; the blade used should be fine enough to prevent the metal being cut from fitting between two teeth.

Sheet cutting is done with the metal resting on the aluminium saw peg. The blade should always be kept perpendicular to the metal being cut, except initially when it is easier to start the cut with the saw leaning forward slightly. To cut round a sharp corner the blade should be rotated slowly on the spot while making four or five strokes or more depending on the thickness of the metal.

For removing enclosed areas such as the centre from an initial D, a hole is first drilled or punched into the portion to be removed and the blade released from the frame at one end, passed through the hole and reclamped so that sawing can proceed as normal.

One of the best ways of preventing saw breakages is to take a good hard look at a blade through a magnifying glass and think that if you were born two hundred years ago you would have had to make the next one yourself before you could continue with the job.

Polishing

When an item such as a ring has had all the work on it completed and the file marks removed with fine emery, the next step is to remove the marks left by the emery paper by polishing.

First the rouge bar is touched on to the rotating finger felt, then on the outside felt, brush and finishing mop. Move the ring up and down the finger felt, taking care not to push it too far up otherwise it will be grabbed and be torn from your fingers, sometimes taking a bit of the finger with it. Take the sharpness off the inside edge of the ring before transferring to the outside felt. This is for the smooth part of the shank only. It has a very fierce polishing action and will take the sharpness off patterned shoulders if allowed to travel that far.

The settings and any engraved or indented parts are polished on the bristle brush which is much less fierce; also the bristles penetrate into the cavities. The brush tends to wear unevenly and in doing so loses some of its polishing ability. When this happens, trim the bristles down more evenly with a pair of scissors or an old electric razor. When they are new the bristles tend to be overlong and soft so they do not polish very quickly. If they are shortened a little initially it will remedy that deficiency.

Finally transfer the ring to the finishing mop. Keep the article moving all the time it is against the mop so that it polishes evenly in all directions. A flat surface if not moved continuously will develop a sort of grain which is very difficult to polish out again.

You get a finer finish if rouge is applied to one half of the mop only and in the final stages move from the rouged to the unrouged half, relying on what rouge has adhered to the article to give the final polish.

The article should be applied to the mop just below the centre line - too high and it will be snatched from your grasp; too low and you cannot see what you are doing.

When the mop is used for the first time, it gives off an immense amount of fluff and continues to do so for the first hour or so of use providing you with an unwanted moustache and beard and black nostrils. This breaking-in period can be shortened considerably if a coarse wire brush is touched on the mop before each use, to remove loose strands and excess fluff.

Small articles that cannot be polished without wearing your finger tips away at the same time, should be held on a piano wire hook and laid against a piece of tough leather. The whole is applied to the mop, making sure that the hook is in no danger of being caught in the mop.

Chain should only be polished in very short sections at a time, otherwise the mop will grab them and snatch them out of your hand. Thin chains will be ruined and heavy watch chains will be whipped around the mop thrashing you around the knuckles until you have the presence of mind to move your hands out of the way and switch off. It is a mistake one rarely makes more than once.

Ear studs with French fittings (a straight wire to take a butterfly clip) are best held by the peg in a pin-vice for polishing.

One final technique is that of removing wrinkles from flat sheet. Cutting sheet with the tin shears nearly always leaves a distorted edge and if it is to be used for something like the base of a flat-backed setting, the wrinkles must be removed so that the bezel can

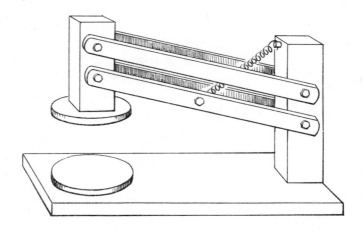

Fig 3.13 A useful machine for planishing sheet, to flatten it and remove wrinkles. The two circular platens, with the sheet between, are slammed together by using the heel of the hand on the top one.

make overall contact for soldering. Hitting with the hammer usually only transfers the wrinkle to another part of the metal. Pressure must be applied to all parts at the same time. One way of doing this is to place it between two flat blocks of metal and giving the top one a hefty blow with the hammer dead-centre. A less crude way is to put it under the press part of the vertical ring-sizing machine and use the lever to hammer it evenly. Finally there is a small machine called a planisher which imitates the action of the ring press in a more convenient way. The two flat parts can be slammed together with the heel of the hand or held together and the top one struck with the hammer (Fig. 3-13).

Chapter 4

General Repairs: Rings

Altering the size of rings must be the job most frequently encountered by the jeweller and one that never ceases to present pitfalls. So, before attempting any work on a ring, examine it thoroughly. The first thing to look for if your work comes from a retailer in repair packets is to make sure that the description on the packet fits the contents. If he has called a three-stoned paste ring a three-stoned diamond ring, query it before going any further or you may get accused of swapping the stones. If a ring has come for sizing only and there is a stone missing or some part damaged and this is not mentioned on the packet, check with the owner first. Otherwise, 'It was alright when I left it' will be a phrase you will become familiar with and you may end up having to do the work for nothing.

When working through a number of packets one tends to take the articles out of the packets to do the neccessary work and put them in a pile ready for polishing, only to find later that you have two or three nearly identical signet rings, or worse, diamond rings and nothing on the packets to tell you which job came out of which packet. It can turn out to be a nasty situation if a customer ends up with the wrong ring, so make a point of putting some identifying information on the packet as you take each article out, such as the initial engraved on a signet or the maker's initials usually stamped next to the hallmark. Names of the main parts of a gem-set ring are given in Fig. 4-1.

The first step in sizing a gem-set or any other ring is to ascertain how many sizes larger or smaller it is to be made. Anything more than three sizes for a gem-set ring - that is, midway up the size stick - is going to put a fair amount of strain on it, usually at the points illustrated in the Figs. 4-2 and 4-3. Examine these for any signs of

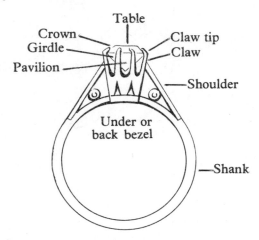

Fig 4.1 Names of the parts of a gem-set ring.

weakness such as a poorly soldered joint or thinness in the casting. If it seems pretty certain that you are going to end up with far more than a sizing job because of a fault, return it and quote for the extra work or otherwise strengthen the weak part with solder before starting the sizing.

The next step will be to heat up the shank of the ring until it darkens, when any previous joins in the shank will show up clearly as a lighter line of solder. But before any heat is applied, one has to make sure that any gemstones in the ring will stand the heat. As a general rule diamonds, rubies and sapphires free from bad flaws will stand any amount of soldering heat provided it builds up and

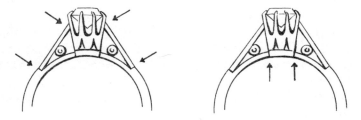

Fig 4.2 (Left) Trying to reduce the size of a gem ring too much strains the parts indicated by the arrows.

Fig 4.3 (Right) If a gem ring is stretched too much, the places where it is likely to be damaged are indicated by the arrows.

dissipates gradually. The 'indestructable diamond' will shatter or go milky white if heated up and dropped in cold water. There is no infallible way for a repairer to indentify gemstones. One becomes familiar with what stones are usually in certain types of setting; as an extreme example, you do not as a rule find pastes or synthetic spinels set in 18ct gold or platinum.

Synthetic rubies and sapphires will stand as much heat as the real thing, so there is no worry there. In the older types of ring what appears to be a ruby or sapphire is quite often a doublet, which is a sandwich having coloured glass on the bottom and a sliver of garnet or quartz fused to the top to withstand the wear (Fig. 4-4). If examined with an eyeglass, the line of the joining can usually be seen running across the side facets as shown. With the much rarer well-cut ones, the join will be around the girdle of the stone and almost undetectable. If the stone is clean, hold it up to the light and look at it from the back with the eyeglass. A doublet will usually show a clear band of purple around the edge of the stone. If you are still in any doubt, touch the back with a needle or similar hard point. If you can mark it, it is glass and the stone a doublet which will not stand any heat.

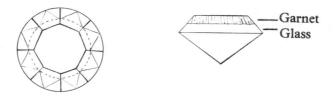

Fig 4.4 A garnet-topped doublet, which looks like a garnet but is paste (glass) with a garnet top.

As for diamonds, most of the common simulants (white synthetic spinel, cubic zirconia [CZ], YAG, white synthetic sapphire) will stand the heat of sizing, so no precautions need be taken. An exception is the natural white zircon.

Some clues to this stone's identity are that it is cut slightly differently from a diamond; the distance between the girdle and the table facet is noticeably greater in the zircon, it gives brighter flashes of colour than a diamond and most conclusive of all it is softer than a diamond and, unless quite new, it nearly always shows signs of wear on the corners of the table facet. A diamond does not show signs of wear. A gemmologist often identifies a zircon by the doubling of the back facet edges when they are viewed through the table of the stone with a lens. See 'Practical Gemmology' by Robert Webster (N.A.G. Press Ltd.). Zircons can also change colour when heated.

Vitreous enamel should be treated like a gemstone. Although it is impervious to acid, it chips and flakes if heated unevenly or stressed in any way.

Garnet will usually stand the heat of sizing, but they have a limit. Almost all other stones will be damaged if heated, not inevitably, but the risk is so great as not to be worth taking. If you are in any doubt about the identity of a gemstone do not take any chances, soak a piece of cotton wool in water and wrap it around the stones before heating the shank. (See Appendix 3).

One alarming phenomenon to be warned of is that a genuine ruby when heated turns green, but thankfully returns to its natural colour as it cools.

Locating Joins

After discovering where the joins are, if any, cut through the one farthest from the head of the ring. There may be another join nearby, indicating that a piece has been added sometime in the past. If the ring has now to be reduced, cut away the added piece or as much as is necessary to reduce the ring to its new size. One size equals 1/16 in or 1.75 mm but this can vary according to the thickness of your saw blade so always err on the short side. It is easier to take out another slice than to stretch the ring if you have reduced it too much. If there is no join in the ring, avoid cutting into the hallmark. If the choice is between cutting into the hallmark or endangering a valuable stone by having the join too near the setting, remove the maker's initials rather than the date letter. In a hundred years time, unless human nature changes, people will be more interested in how old the ring is rather than who made it and in the case of most modern peg-set jewellery you will be doing the manufacturer a favour.

With the piece removed, the gap has now to be closed. Grip the shank in the ring pliers just below the shoulder as shown in Fig. 4-5 and, supporting the shoulder with the finger, bend the ring a little then move the pliers a little nearer the gap and bend again. Continue doing this until the gap is half closed with the ring bending in a nice even curve. Then transfer the pliers to the other side of the

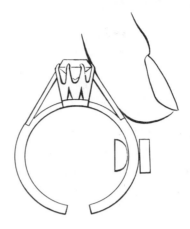

ring and repeat the process until the gap is closed. Check the size on the size stick. The ring will not be perfectly round. There is usually a slight gap under each shoulder where your finger has prevented any bending from taking place. Allow half a size for this, that is: assume that the ring will be half a size larger when properly rounded. If it appears that it will be the correct size and the ends of the shank meet squarely, the next step is to rejoin the ring with suitable solder. If the ends do not meet squarely, insert a flat parallel-sided needle file in the join and move it up and down a few times. Alternatively hold the gap closed and run the saw blade through it. Once is usually enough to square up the faces.

Close the gap completely, but do not leave it under pressure. You should be able to pull it apart with the slightest effort. This is even more important if there is another join nearby; if there is any pressure on the join, as soon as the solder reaches melting point the piece will fly out.

Coat the join with flux all the way round then, holding the ring with the join uppermost, place a panel of solder over it. If the ring has heat-sensitive stones in it, wrap them in wet cotton wool again before applying the heat. Do not hold the ring square on to the flame but allow the flame to strike diagonally across the join and move it from one side of the join to the other, endeavouring to bring them both to the right temperature simultaneously (Fig. 4-6). When the flame is first applied the flux will usually turn white and swell, sometimes flicking off the piece of solder, so keep the tip of the tweezers resting gently on the panel of solder until the flux has settled down, but make sure the tweezers are clean and free of

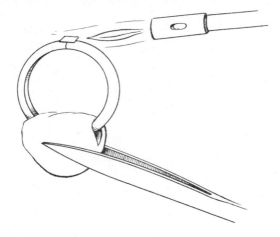

Fig 4.6 Soldering a shank with the stone protected by wet cotton wool.

flux or you may find the solder stuck to the tweezers instead of the join when you remove them.

If the gods are smiling on you, when the solder reaches melting point it will roll up into a ball and be drawn into the join. If it runs on to one side only, move the flame a little over to the opposite side and try to ease the solder over with the tip of the tweezers. If it does not work at the first attempt, take the flame away, reflux the join and put another piece of solder in place, but with the bulk of it on the unsoldered side, and try again. If you keep trying with the tweezers, the solder and ring will become too hot and merge together and no amount of prodding with the tweezers will get the join soldered.

With the join satisfactorily soldered, allow the ring to cool down then, after removing the cotton wool, place the ring in the sulphuric acid pickle for a few minutes.

If the ring contains pearls, coral or a shell cameo, it should not be put bodily into the acid or these stones will be spoilt. In these cases, and any others you have doubts about, put the ring on a saucer or plastic lid and apply acid to the discoloured parts with a matchstick.

After the acid has had time to work, rinse the ring thoroughly in clean water and dry it with an absorbent tissue. Examine the join to make sure the solder flows right through to the inside of the ring. Sometimes it does not and this fact is obscured by the flux and not discovered until the ring has been pickled. In this case, reflux the join and heat the ring from the inside until the solder flows right through.

If the join is sound, remove the excess solder from the inside of the ring with the tip of the ringmaker's file, then place the ring on the triblet. Holding it hard against the taper, tap with the mallet any parts that are not in contact with the triblet. With an extra thick ring you may have to resort to the hammer in order to get the ring properly rounded, but remember every hammer blow will leave a mark that will have to be filed out afterwards.

With claw-set rings, the rounding-up process sometimes lifts the claws adjacent to the shoulders. Check for this next and burnish down with the flat of the tweezers or large graining tool any that are off the stone. To make certain that they are in contact with the stone, drag the claws over a woollen jumper. Any faulty claws will be found to have a collection of hairs caught under them.

Finally remove any excess solder and hammer marks from the outside of the ring with the file, using the action described in the section on filing, and finish the inside and outside with the emery sticks.

Enlarging a Ring

Enlarging a ring is a much more difficult job for the beginner as it takes a fair amount of practice to get the piece being added to stay in position while being soldered because the metals expand as they are heated and the flux hardens and moves the piece being added before the solder has had time to melt.

After taking any necessary precautions with gemstones, heat the ring to reveal any joins. If a small piece has been added previously, it is usually best to cut this out and replace it with one larger piece. The fewer joins in the shank the stronger it is and the easier to work on. After checking that there are no weak spots under the head (see Fig. 4-3), saw it through and open it up gradually with the ring pliers, reversing the action used for making the ring smaller. Sometimes - if there is a pattern on the outside of the ring for instance - it is better to force the cut ring up the triblet with the fingers until it has reached the correct size. This action puts pressure on the claws adjacent to the shoulders just as the reverse is the case when making a ring smaller. On rings with long slender claws this can sometimes result in the stone becoming tilted in the setting, so watch out for that.

When the ring has reached the correct size on the size stick, select a piece of shank wire slightly larger in section than the ring shank to fill the gap. If it is slightly larger it will allow for a certain amount of movement when the ring is heated and leave something to file when matching it to the existing shank. If a piece is used that is an exact match to the shank, it needs extreme care when cleaning up the joins to avoid ending with a thin section in the shank. Curve the piece of shank wire to match the curve of the ring and span it across the gap with the ring still on the size stick. Then mark with a scriber where it will have to be cut (Fig. 4-7). Saw it off on the 'spare' side of the mark, file off any burrs, and try it for fit in

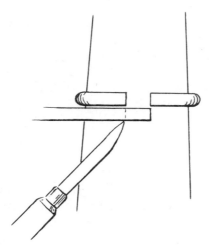

Fig 4.7 Measuring the length of new shank to be inserted in a ring being made larger.

the gap in the ring. The piece should be a light friction fit in the gap. If it has to be forced in, it will spring out again or move when heated. The faces should match up as perfectly as you can make them, as indicated in Figs. 4-8, 4-9 and 4-10, the solder will fill any small inaccuracies but there is much less likelihood of the piece moving when heated if it is a good fit.

The next step is to solder one of the joins. Never try to solder both at the same time because the small piece you are adding will inevitably become hot first and the solder will flow on to that and not in the joins. After fluxing both joins and placing a piece of solder over one as in Fig. 4-11, heat the shank on that side first and gradually move the flame up to the join, endeavouring to get that side of the shank and the sizing piece up to the solder's melting point at the same time. If the join solders alright but the sizing

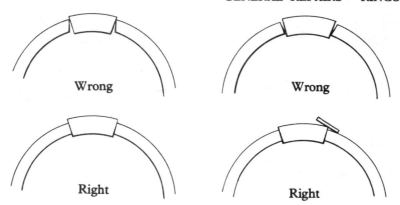

Fig 4.8 (Top, left) An insert in a shank cannot be soldered effectively if it 'fits' like this.

Fig 4.9 (Right) It is equally ineffective to try soldering an insert that fits like this.

Fig 4.10 (Above, left) A correctly placed insert, which is slightly oversize in width and is an accurate friction fit.

Fig 4.11 (Right) A tiny piece of solder correctly placed for soldering one join.

piece moves out of alignment, do not be tempted to correct it with the tweezers; leave it and let the ring cool down. With sufficient experience it is possible to realign it while keeping the solder molten, but to begin with it is better left as it is and the other join lined up ready for soldering. With the second join one proceeds as for reducing a ring with the flame diagonally across the join. If this join solders successfully, and the other is misaligned, saw through the first one, realign it and resolder it.

After pickling, rinsing and drying, the excess metal is filed away from the inside of the ring; then it is shaped up and filed the same as for reducing. Take great care when filing the piece down; it is easy to take off too much and you cannot put it back on again. The only solution is to cut the piece out and start all over again.

The process is the same for all kinds of rings that are midway up the size stick (sizes M.N.O.) and the alteration is three, or, at the most, four sizes. When more than that amount is to be taken out or put into a ring, it is not possible to make it round without causing some distortion to the head and shoulders. The flat surface of a signet ring will become bowed or concave and the settings of gem rings will become distorted and unsafe. In these instances the ring has to be left oval to some degree and the finished size ascertained by fitting it to one of your own fingers of known size, using the finger size rings as described earlier.

Expansion Rates

There are two booby traps to watch out for in the ring world. One is known as the two-tone wedding ring and consists of a yellow gold inner band with a narrower white gold or platinum outer band soldered to it. Sometimes they are the same width but the white gold is very thin with an engraved pattern cutting through it into the yellow. The metals themselves would stretch a little but the solder holding them together won't, so try it at your peril. Reducing them appears to be a simple job, allowing for the fact that the white gold solder you are likely to use will show up on the yellow half of the ring. You cut out the piece, close the gap, flux it, put the solder in place and start to heat it. It is at that point that things start to go wrong. The expansion rate of the yellow gold is much greater than that of white, with the consequence that the join springs apart as soon as the heat is applied, and the more the heat the larger the gap. The only way to get the join soldered is to hold the ends together by force. Tweezers are not strong enough; only an old pair of pliers with a semi-circle filed out of each jaw to take the curve of the ring will hold it together. A pair of snipe-nosed pliers with the jaws softened and bent as shown in Fig. 4-12 will also do.

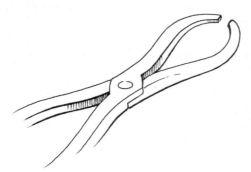

Fig 4.12 To resolder a two-tone (two part) ring that has separated, a special tool is needed to hold the parts together. This one is made by bending the jaws of a pair of snipe-nosed pliers.

The other trap is the hollow ring. These are usually old gypsy style rings and are identical to their solid counterpart in every way except for weight, and even that is not a foolproof guide because the hollow is sometimes filled with wax or plaster which, though it does not bring the weight up to that of a solid one, is sufficient to fool you if you are not looking for it.

Any that seem the least suspicious should be examined for any small dents, which do not occur in solid rings. Another check is that they are usually put together in halves and with age the soldered seam becomes visible. So examine the outside edges with the eyeglass. If there is a hole right through the head to take a stone and it has not been lined with a piece of tube, you can look into it from the back and see if it is hollow. If you are still in any doubt, wrap the head in cotton wool and warm the shank to expose the seam.

In some the head only is hollow and these can sometimes be sized if the alteration is not too great, but the completely hollow ones cannot even be gripped with the pliers without damaging them.

Sometimes, when a ring is too small or too heavy for the wet cotton wool to keep a heat-sensitive stone cool long enough for the solder to melt, the stone will have to be removed from the setting while the work is carried out and reset afterwards. As soon as the cotton wool begins to dry out, take it out of the flame and cool the shank quickly by dabbing it on another piece of wet cotton wool or holding it against the aluminium sawing peg before the heat remaining in the shank can travel up to the stone. Do not be tempted to re-wet the cotton wool covering the stone or you may shatter it.

Removing and resetting claw set stones is relatively simple. All that is needed is a very sharp knife to get under the claw tip and lift it off the stone. While doing this, support the body of the claw on the bench peg as shown in Fig. 4-13 so that the whole of the claw will not be forced outwards. Remember that the claws will have to be bent back again later so bend as few of the claws as possible and by a minimal amount to lessen the risk of any breaking off.

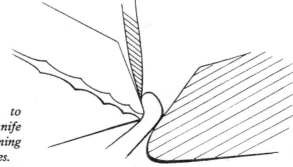

Fig 4.13 Where to insert a sharp knife when straightening claws to unset stones.

With the stone out and the soldering completed, it is as well to wave the torch lightly over the claw tips, bringing them to a dull red to soften them and reduce the risk of their cracking or breaking off when bent back again.

Bezel Settings

A continuous bezel setting is a little more difficult and needs greater care to avoid damaging the setting or the stone. Again the knife blade must be very sharp and with a curved tip as shown in Fig. 4-14. This type of setting is mostly confined to cabochon-cut stones. Garnets and the quartz group of stones: amethyst, tiger eye, agate, etc, are fairly tough and will stand the pressure of the knife blade, but opals are extremely fragile and on no account should any pressure be put on them. Treat them as if they were pieces of glass for they break and chip just as easily.

Fig 4.14 Removing a cabochon stone from a closed bezel setting, using a sharp knife blade with a curved tip.

First examine the setting with the eyeglass to see if there is a gap anywhere between the stone and the setting to give you a start with the knife blade. If not, and the setting is oval, insert the tip of the blade in the least curved portion of the setting as shown because it will bend easiest at that point. Roll the knife down to get more of the curved part under the setting and, with the ring resting against the peg, push the setting away from the stone a little then move the knife blade along the gap you have made and repeat. Do not try to lift a portion of the setting clear of the stone in one go; it may tear or crack. Do a little at a time, working your way around the stone two or three times until the stone is free.

With claw settings as well as this type, avoid using the edge of the stone as a lever for the knife blade, flaws are often concealed beneath a claw or bezel setting and pressure on these are likely to cause the stone to chip or crack across.

Soften the bezel when the sizing work is completed and if you have any cracks in it, run the fine saw blade (4/0) through them to clean them then fill with the appropriate solder.

To reset the stone, use the broad end of a pair of tweezers and with a rolling motion, as shown in Fig. 4-15 work your way around the stone two or three times. Again do not try to press one spot completely down before moving on to the next because you will end up with wrinkles in the bezel that are almost impossible to remove.

Fig 4.15 Resetting a stone in a bezel. A side of the handle end of a pair of tweezers is used with a rocking action.

When you have got the bezel as far down on to the stone as you can by this method, there is nearly always a small gap left due to the springiness of the metal. That final gap can be closed in two ways, first by using the edge of the tweezers as a burnisher rubbing it backwards and forwards and pressing down at the same time. Position the setting on the peg so that only the corner of the tweezers does the pressing and the peg used as a guide to keep the tweezers in position and prevent them touching the stone (Fig. 4-16).

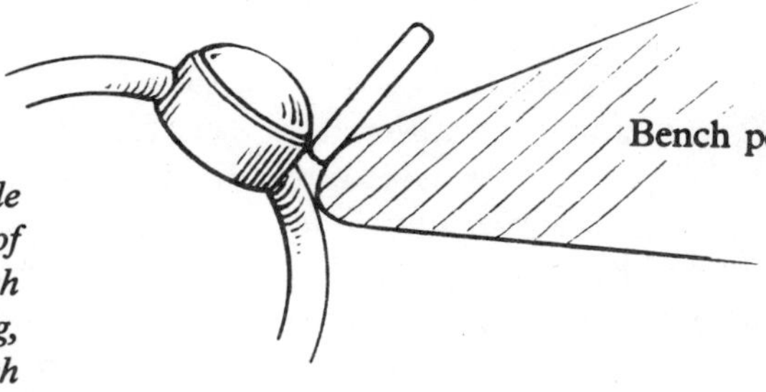

Fig 4.16 Using the side of the handle end of tweezers to burnish round a bezel setting, taking care not to touch the stone.

Bench peg

The other method used to close that final gap is to run the millgraining tool all around the edge. This breaks the edge up into minute beads which spread outwards on to the stone. For larger settings the ring is best held in the rings clamps as this enables you to turn the ring more easily as you move around the setting with the milligrainer. Begin on the straightest portion of the setting, if it is oval, and roll the wheel backwards and forwards for about ⅛ in with light pressure until the beads are fully formed. Keep to the outer edge of the setting as in Fig. 4-17 because the wheel is extremely hard and will score most stones if it comes into contact with them.

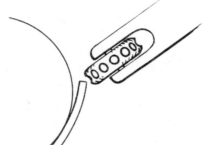

Fig 4.17 Closing a bezel setting by using a milligrain tool. The wheel of this forms little beads all round the setting.

When the first section is complete, move on to the next, keeping the wheel in contact with the beads so that you have an uninterrupted line of beads. If you slip or take the wheel off, begin again by lightly rolling the wheel over the existing beads making sure that the beads fall into the cavities in the wheel and are not cut in half because of misalignment. Continue like this all the way round the stone until the setting is in contact with it. To check that the stone is actually gripped by the setting, hold the ring upside down, the stone facing the floor, and tap the stone lightly with your finger tip. If it is still loose, you will hear a distinct click. Mill the setting once again until the click goes.

The sizing information applies to all metals commonly used in jewellery with two exceptions: with a heat-sensitive stone set in silver it is useless to wrap it in wet cotton wool. Silver is such a good conductor of heat that the wool will have dried out and burnt long before the solder can melt. The only alternatives are to use a highly concentrated source of heat such as oxy-acetylene or remove the stone from the ring.

There are many gold-plated silver rings about with real stones in them that look very much like the 9ct counterpart they are made to imitate. Check the hallmark carefully before heating. They are usually stamped .925 or just 'Silver' but some have the silver hallmark which, at a quick glance can be taken for the 9ct hallmark. Even if you take the stones out in order to size these rings, you are bound to cut through the plating when filing or polishing them. To gild them would be a waste of time as it would wear off within days. The best procedure with these is to send them back with an explanation and an estimate and hope they do not return.

The other exception applies to platinum rings. Unless you have a separate set of felts and mops and the special rouge it is not possible to get a satisfactory polish on platinum. Whether you use 18ct white gold hard solder or platinum solder (it is sometimes necessary to use the former because of its lower melting point), you usually end up polishing some of the solder out of the join before the platinum begins to shine and the join becomes very obvious. The way to avoid this is by using polishing paper round the inside emery stick and to polish the inside of the ring by imitating the movement of the finger felt. It will not take long to achieve a bright finish. Again it is best to use a worn piece of paper for the final rub. Repeat on the outside but instead of using a stick, hold the paper across your fingers and move the ring up and down in the gap betweeen two fingers so that the paper is in contact with the front and sides of the shank at the same time. If the finish is still a little foggy, a very light rub on the rouge mop will brighten it.

New Shanks

When replacing a worn out shank, the joins are going to be high up the sides of the ring next to the shoulders so the heat has a very short distance to travel to reach any heat-sensitive stones. With 18ct gold rings, wet cotton wool will usually keep the stones cool enough because 18ct is not such a good conductor of heat. But 9ct gold is alloyed with nearly two-thirds copper and silver which are both good conductors of heat, so the cotton wool treatment does not always work. It is worth a try though, before resorting to the risky business of removing the stones from their settings. But give it up as soon as the cotton wool begins to dry out.

Before cutting away the worn section of the shank, check the ring size and your instructions. Sometimes you are told to fit a new shank the same size as the present one and, after you have cut the old one off, it is not so easy to assess what the size was.

Heat the ring slightly on the shoulders to make certain that it has not had a new shank fitted in the past. If joins show that the ring has been reshanked, cut the old one off at the shoulder side of the joins even if the existing shank has not worn that far. You do not want four joins in the shank even if you were lucky enough to solder a new one on to the stub ends of the old one without the whole thing falling to pieces.

Clean off any old solder that may have escaped the saw and square off the ends with the file. Sometimes, particularly with signet rings, you may find one shoulder worn very thin where it has rubbed against another ring on the adjacent finger in which case you will have to put a long lap joint on that side in order to thicken it up again.

Select a piece of shank wire thick enough to match up to the ring, slightly oversize rather than under, and bend it with the ring pliers until it matches the correct size on the size stick without any gaps. Place the ring head on the stick with one side resting against the squared off end of the shank wire and mark with a scriber where the shank wire is to be cut off (Fig. 4-18). Saw off the new shank on the waste side of the line and square that end to match the head. Hold the halves of the ring together round the size stick to make sure the size will be correct and that the ends match reasonably well. Flux all four faces to be soldered and melt a piece of easy solder on to one side of the ring head. I said 'easy solder' because if there are any soldered joins on the head you are in less danger of melting them.

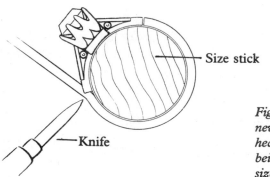

Size stick

Knife

Fig 4.18 Fitting a whole new shank to a ring head. Here the length is being marked using a size stick and a scriber.

Find the most comfortable way of holding the halves together in the tweezers so that you can apply the heat to the proposed join without getting any other part of the ring hot and the halves can be held together in the tweezers without slipping as in Fig. 4-19. Avoid having the flame strike an inside surface of the tweezers because it will be deflected down towards the fingers and you will be forced to drop everything and start again when the tweezers have cooled.

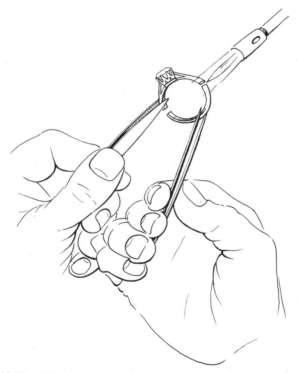

Fig 4.19 To solder in a new shank, fix the torch tightly in a vice or elsewhere to free both hands, one of which holds the head and the other the shank, both in tweezers.

With the halves of the ring in separate tweezers, bring your hands together so that they touch somewhere. This steadies the hands and gives you a fulcrum or pivot point enabling you to bring the halves of the join accurately together. Practise bringing the two halves together a few times before applying the heat, and press them together lightly to check that neither is likely to slip in the tweezers at the crucial moment. Holding the two halves in contact apply the flame to the shank first so that it will be slightly hotter than the head when the solder is brought to melting point - that way you make use of the fact that the solder will move towards the hottest part of the metal. As soon as the solder flows, lower the join from the flame and hold it there for a second while the solder solidifies and the heat dissipates from the shank. As when enlarging a ring, do not worry if the join is not accurately lined up. Now the ring is in one piece it is easy to line up and solder the second join accurately, then cut and resolder the first if necessary.

If possible, any excess metal on the section of the new shank should be on the outside of the ring where it is easier to file away (Fig. 4-20).

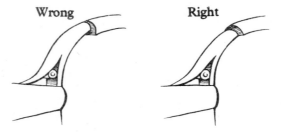

Fig 4.20 Excess metal on an inserted piece should be on the outside, as on the right, not as on the left, to make it easier to file away.

With the join satisfactorily soldered, pickle and dry the ring. Then file away any excess metal and solder from the inside of the joins. Place the ring on the triblet and round it up; then check that the size is right. If it is a fraction too small, give the shank a series of light hammer blows while pressing the ring against the taper of the triblet. If you cannot get it up to size, anneal the shank, taking care not to melt the joins, and try again, or stretch it on the gem ring sizing machine. When you have got it to the right size, anneal the shank again to take any stress off the joins. If the ring has ended up too large, you will have to cut through one of the joins, remove a bit of the shank and rejoin it.

When the size is right and the inside round and smooth, file away the excess from the outside using the rolling motion described earlier until the new shank matches the existing pieces of the old one. File away until the ring looks right and in proportion.

Do not be tempted just to clean up the joins and leave too much metal on the new shank. When finished it should look like a new ring, not like an old one with a thick shank fitted.

One is sometimes given a ring to be reshanked that has heat-sensitive stones that the wet cotton wool cannot protect and the stones cannot be removed and reset economically, such as an antique pearl and turquoise cluster. To remove the stones you would either break off the grains or break the stones or both. In these cases the only way to make the ring wearable is to fit a new shank with soft solder-assisted joins. First the new shank is rounded up and made the right size then a flap of sheet is hard soldered to each end as shown in Fig. 4-21. Curve the sheet to match the underside of the shoulders accurately then soft solder them into position. Finally remove any excess sheet from each side of the shoulder and be careful not to polish the soft solder or the joins will show and be weakened slightly.

Fig 4.21 It is impossible to hard solder a new shank to a head set with heat-sensitive stones that cannot be removed or protected. If the customer is adamant on a repair, the only solution is to use soft solder, but then the ring is legally not gold and must not bear a hallmark, or be sold as gold in the U.K.

Claw Tips

Before doing any soldering work on the head of a ring, always anneal the shank first. Even if it has not been stretched on a sizing machine in the past, the friction of being worn builds up a little tension and if this is not removed to begin with, any joins in the head will spring apart when heated, creating a lot of unnecessary work.

Most claw tipping work is done on engagement rings which, being worn all the time, wear quickly. As the claws are the most prominent part, they get the most wear.

The six claw solitaire is the easiest to retip so I will begin with that, but first I will make a distinction between retipping and rebuilding claws. By retipping I mean strengthening an existing claw tip with solder. Rebuilding means removing the remnants of any tip and fitting a new one.

Often the whole of a claw tip is still in existence but is paper thin, in which case it is a relatively simple task to melt a panel of solder of the appropriate colour on to it, heating it until it rolls a short way down the body of the claw as shown in Fig. 4-22. Sometimes it works so well that the only finishing required is to polish the ring, but if too much of the solder remains on the top it has to be filed down with the needle file and reshaped, otherwise its prominence will make it vulnerable to being knocked away from the stone.

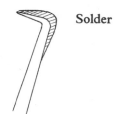

Solder

Fig 4.22 Strengthening a worn claw tip with solder.

Sometimes a ring will arrive with a stone out, but the claws worn on one side of the setting only. In this case it is sometimes possible to stretch the remains of the worn claws sufficiently to bend them over the stone so that only retipping is necessary. To stretch them, the top millimetre or so is gripped in the flat pliers and squeezed and pulled upwards at the same time. An old pair of pliers with the sharp edges worn off is best for this job. New ones tend to bite too sharply and break off the stretched piece. Apart from the fact that less work is involved by doing it this way, the claws match up to the existing ones better.

If the claw tips are completely worn away it will be necessary to rebuild them with new metal. If the stone is still in the setting, even if it is not heat-sensitive, it is safer to remove it while the tips are being soldered in place and reset it afterwards. As mentioned before, diamonds, rubies and sapphires free from bad flaws will stand heating up to red if the process is done gradually, but never take unnecessary risks, particularly if the stone is one you could ill afford to replace if anything goes wrong.

There are protective coatings one can apply to these stones before heating, one is a paste of boric acid crystals mixed with methylated spirits. I used it for a while but abandoned it as too messy. I have rarely had a stone damaged by heat. It has usually happened by sudden cooling, when it has slipped from the tweezers and landed on something cold. Large sapphires sometimes lose their polish when heated but large sapphires are expensive so you would normally avoid heating them anyway.

Once the stone is removed, file away any remnants of the tips down to the lip on which the girdle of the stone rests, then file the top of each claw at an angle so that when the new tip is soldered in place it will form a lap join as shown in Fig. 4-23.

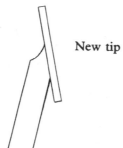

New tip

Fig 4.23 Retipping a claw by soldering on a piece of new metal, using a lap joint.

Preparing New Tips

Next cut a number of tips from sheet metal of the appropriate material or better still from a piece of flattened round wire as this is easier to grip in the tweezers. It is best to use the same metal that the setting is made from but 18ct white gold will solder on to platinum with white gold solder and the difference is undetectable when finished.

Always cut one or two more tips than are actually needed because they flick from the tweezers easily and it is annoying to have to stop half way through the job to cut more.

When the tops of the claws have been fluxed, stick a small panel of solder on to each one then waft the setting gently through the torch flame until the flux ceases to boil. If any solder drops off, reflux that claw, apply another piece of solder and warm as before. When each claw has a piece of solder securely stuck in place, grip the ring in the tweezers in the left hand as shown in Fig. 4-24, then pick up a tip in the tweezers in the other hand.

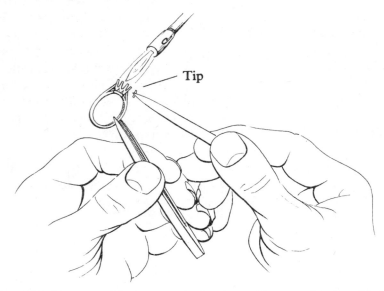

Fig 4.24 How to solder a new tip in place using two hands with the torch fixed.

Have the flux brush propped somewhere handy and touch the tip on to it then bring the hands together as shown so that they steady each other as illustrated. Melt the nearest piece of solder and, just as it begins to run, bring the new tip into the flame. As soon as it is hot, place it on the melted solder in the position shown and release it. If the solder has run on to the tip, lower it from the flame immediately. If you keep the solder fluid for too long, the weight of the new tip will cause it to slide down the claw and you will have the tricky job of pushing it back into place again. Proceed in this way until all six tips are in place then, when it is cool, drop the ring in the pickle.

For this job you should have the flame turned down so that if possible it heats only one claw at a time, but not so small that it takes a long time to heat the solder, otherwise oxides may develop that prevent the solder from running.

When the ring is rinsed and dried, check that all the tips are securely soldered and resolder any that look weak. If the tips are not too hefty to bend, put the stone back in the setting and press the claws half way down, just enough to hold the stone in place. Then, using the knife edge needle file, file the tops to a blunt point and file away the sides of the tip until they match the existing claws.

Remove the projecting tail of the tip until it is flush with the claw, then press the tips fully down on to the stone. Match the claws and file them back if they are too long, with the smooth edge of the file resting against the stone. Do not be tempted to leave them overlong to hold the stone better. They are more likely to be caught and bent back if too long. They should not project more than half way up the side facets at the most on very small stones, as in Fig. 4-25, and much less than that on larger stones.

The decision of whether or not to set a faceted stone with the claws on the kite facet or where the two smaller facets meet, is mostly a matter of personal choice. When the claw is bent over the stone, there are gaps beneath the claw in both instances. In either case it is possible to burnish the metal over the gaps by finishing off with a large diameter graining tool in a twisting and rolling motion.

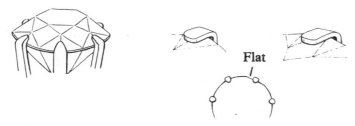

Flat

Fig 4.25 Tips should not be too long otherwise they will snag and be more likely to break off.

Often the decision is made by the need to cover a flaw on the stone's edge. Diamonds in particular are considered worth cutting and polishing even with a large one in this position.

The fault is usually one of three types, a small flat on the circumference of the stone which can be well disguised by positioning the claw at its centre as shown, a black carbon spot inside the stone which again can be hidden or disguised, and a small crack or cavity. In the last case, great care must be taken not to put any pressure on the crack or allow a hard tool to press against it or you may break a the stone in two.

If the tips still feel rough after filing or are not tight on the stone, place the tip of a large graining tool over them and roll it round under light pressure until they are smooth and flush with the stone.

One common fault with new tips is that sometimes they do not bend at a point level with the girdle of the stone because a fillet of solder has made them too thick at that point. They end up looking as shown in Fig. 4-26. Make sure there is not too much solder at that point before setting the stone.

Fig 4.26 A badly fitting retipped claw, which has bent above girdle level owing to the excess solder (shaded).

Whether the ring is to have the claws retipped or rebuilt and whether the ring is a single stone, three-stone or cluster, the procedure is the same.

On some settings the claws are in pairs (Fig. 4-27). With these it is best to treat each pair as a single claw using one large tip for both claws. Split and file them when all the soldering is completed. If you try to put individual tips on them, almost always they come into contact and solder together.

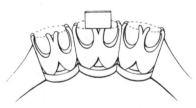

Fig 4.27 If claws are in pairs, it is best to retip them as one and then file out two claws.

Square Settings

Square settings holding square stones usually have the claws as a small right angle on each corner as shown in Fig. 4-28. When these are worn, remove the stone and file the claws down to the ledge that supports the stone and replace them with new right angle pieces. Before attempting to bend them on to the stone file a 'V' notch in the corner of each angle, which leaves a neater finish and

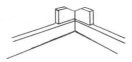

Fig 4.28 When making a new claw for a square setting, file a notch in the corner so that the metal can be bent over more easily and will give a neat finish.

makes the metal easier to bend over. Remember that the corners of square stones, even hard stones, break off easily, so use the minimum of pressure on them and burnish the last bit down rather than press it. Emeralds are often found in this type of setting. They are almost as brittle as opals, so extreme care must be taken when resetting them.

Some older type diamond rings have mill grained settings which are just circular bezels finished with a mill grain tool. They are not often worn completely away and can be thickened up with solder. If there are any places where the setting has worn completely off the stone, the gap can usually be bridged with a piece of metal then filed to shape (after it has been soldered in place - not before). Occasionally the end settings on three and five stone half hoops are beyond even this treatment, in which case the bezels will have to be replaced with either a short length of tube or a circle made from flat strip. If flat strip is used, be sure to use a hard grade of solder to join the circle before soldering it to the ring or the solder will run out of the join when heated the second time.

Three and five stone half hoops with what are often called carved settings containing heat-sensitive stones, usually opals, are more troublesome to deal with because of the difficulty of removing and resetting the stones. They usually have claws on the outside edges and grains pushed over the stones between the settings. The claws present no problem because, if they need to be rebuilt, they can be filed away to free the stone. Raising the grains without breaking them off demands a great deal of care and patience using a chisel-edge graver. If you are unfortunate enough to break one off, or have to cut one off to avoid damaging a stone, the best way to replace it is to drill a small hole where it was and tightly wedge a bit of round wire in the hole before soldering it so that it will remain in place while the new claws are being fitted even if the solder does melt again.

91

If you get one of these rings with just one missing claw to be replaced, the safest way of doing it is to file a groove into the remaining stump. Shape up a new claw to fit snugly in the groove with the tip curved to rest against the stone. Then soft solder it into the groove. For added security put a spot of super-glue (cyanoacrylate) between the claw and the stone. As this is something of a compromise, it should be explained to the customer first.

The sides and back bezels of gem rings become badly worn and undercut when worn next to wedding rings and, as I mentioned earlier, the shank is subject to the same wear so that more often than not a ring needs both these points attending to at the same time.

With three or five stone half hoops, the centre setting is usually the largest and receives the most wear, sometimes being completely worn through at the base while the adjacent settings have only small flats worn on them. See Fig. 4-29. If that is the case, the back bezel will have to be rebuilt with a piece of flat gold wire on each side. The base of the claw, if that is worn away too - should be rebuilt with white gold or platinum using an easy grade of solder. The flats on the remaining settings, if worn less than half way through, can usually be rounded up again with a blob of solder.

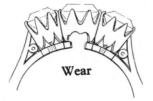

Fig 4.29 The centre setting of a three- or five-stone ring usually receives most wear on the base, which will have to be rebuilt, using easy solder.

To build up the base of the centre setting, the remains of the yellow gold back bezel are cleaned up and levelled with a needle file and a small piece of easy solder melted on to each stump. Select a piece of gold slightly thicker and wider than the original bezel because you will lose a bit when rounding it up with the file later. Flux the piece and lay it across the gap with the top edge level with the top of the stumps. Any excess should be on the inside of the ring, not near the base of the claw where it will be difficult to file down later. Hold the ring in tweezers in the left hand and, with the tip of the tweezers in the right hand, hold the new piece in position. The hands should touch each other somewhere to steady them. Heat up the setting again but do not allow any of the flame to strike the new piece directly or it will probably melt before the solder. As soon as the solder melts, sufficient heat will be conducted to the new piece and bring it to solder heat almost instantaneously. You will see it drop on to the stumps and the solder flush round the edges.

If it is slightly askew, touch it with the tip of the tweezers while the solder is molten, but do not keep the heat on it too long or the solder holding the setting together will melt and sometimes fill up the spaces between the claws. It is better to leave it slightly askew and try to true it up later with the file than risk overheating the setting.

Worn Claw Bases

If the base of the claw has worn so much that it does not reach the piece just added, that gap will have to be bridged too. First, a piece of white gold easy solder is melted on to the worn end of the claw base and a piece of white gold or platinum placed in position with the bottom just touching the new piece added. It does not matter if the flame hits white gold or platinum because they cannot be melted with a propane flame, so this part is a little more simple. After this piece is soldered in position, it only remains to solder the two new pieces together. See Fig. 4-30. Use a very small piece of 9ct yellow easy solder. Its lower melting point will prevent any of the previous joins melting and the pieces moving out of position. Repeat the process on the other side of the ring. Do not attempt any filing until all the soldering is completed. When the job is pickled and dried, file away the excess metal until the setting looks like new. If the bases of the other settings have been rounded up

Fig 4.30 The base of a claw may be so badly worn that it requires two new pieces soldered on to each side.

with solder, file them too until the solder blends with the setting and cannot be detected.

When there is not much difference between the size of the centre setting and the side settings, the back bezels of the side settings will usually have worn too much to be built up with solder alone. In this case, a piece of flattened wire bent to match the curve of the ring is soldered across all three or five of the back bezels as in Fig. 4-31. This is divided up later into individual back bezels by notching with a three cornered file and rounding up. If the ring is to have a new shank as well, the old shank can sometimes be used to build up the back bezels as long as it has no joins in it.

Fig 4.31 (Left) If the settings of a three- or five-stone ring are of about the same size, they can wear more evenly and can be repaired by soldering on a single strip which is later notched with a file.

Clusters and cross-over rings become worn in the same way by being constantly rubbed against a wedding ring. These two styles tend to tilt and allow the wedding ring to slide under them so that wear is usually confined to the back bezel and in the cross-over the bulge of the shoulder. The worn area is usually concave where it has taken on the outline of the wedding ring. It has to be cleaned and any irregularities removed with the half-round or rat-tail needle file. It is built up with a piece of half-round shank wire as shown in Figs. 4-32 and 4-33. Any excess is filed away.

Fig 4.32 (Left) Wear on the side of a cluster ring caused by rubbing on another ring.

Fig 4.33 (Right) By soldering on a length of half-round shank wire, which is later filed to shape.

Chapter 5

Making a Ring

Fairly frequently a batch of repairs includes a loose stone which is to be mounted as a ring. Usually a sketch and a quotation is required, so it is worthwhile spending a little time sketching some basic designs for round, oval and octagonal ring mounts and having the sheet photocopied. When this job crops up, you can then indicate the mounts applicable and put a price beside them.

If you have managed to master the work in the previous chapters, making a ring should present no problems at all. Even if you do make a bloomer, it is your own material you are working on so no-one but you is going to be upset.

Ready-made claw settings are available for most sizes of round stone from about 2.5 mm upwards. It is worthwhile keeping a stock of the smaller ones. Being light in weight, they do not represent a great outlay and the manufacturing costs are such that it is not worth making them by hand. The larger they are, the heavier they become and more expensive. However, being larger they are easier of make by hand.

A six-pronged claw setting to take a quarter carat diamond should not present any difficulties. I specified diamond because carat is a unit of weight and the size and diameter varies for different kinds of stones of the same weight.

A tool that can be a great help in forming the taper on round and other shapes of setting is the collet plate and punch in Fig. 5-1. The punch is tapered to a point and the plate has a series of holes of various sizes with a matching taper. They are available in round, oval and octagonal shapes.

A quarter carat diamond is usually 4.5 mm in diameter so the strip of metal to make the claw will have to be 3.142 times 4.5 = 14.14 mm. Round that up to 15 mm to allow for truing up the join.

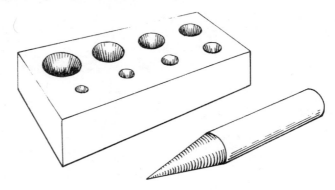

Fig 5.1 A collet plate and punch for forming a taper on round settings of certain sizes. These are also available for oval and octagonal shapes.

The strip should be about 0.5 mm thick and 4.5 mm wide. Bend it into a cylinder with the round-nosed pliers then, with the ends pressed together, run the saw blade between them (Fig. 5-2) so that they match up. Then completely close up the gap and solder it with a hard grade of solder. Check that the stone just enters the cylinder.

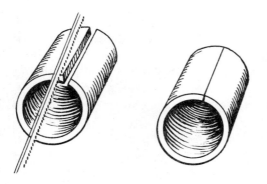

Fig 5.2 Squaring the ends of a tube. With them pressed together, run a saw blade between them and then press them close together for soldering.

After pickling it, place the cylinder in a hole in the collet plate, so that about half of it is above the surface of the plate, then hammer it in so that it takes on the taper of the hole. The tapered holes in the back of an old draw plate can be used as an alternative to the collet plate. Check that the stone will just enter the wide end. If not, open it up a little by putting it back in the hole, placing the tip of a round punch into it, and tapping the punch with the hammer until the hole is the right size.

The next job is to form the claws by cutting the gaps between them. A gapping file can be used for this. It is the same as a flat needle file, but the edges are rounded and only they have teeth; the flats are smooth. If you do not have a gapping file the right size, a rat-tail will do the job if you use just a small portion of it so that it does not jam on the forward stroke.

Divide the top edge of the setting into six equal portions and mark them with a knife blade. With the gapping file or the rat-tail file a shallow groove equidistant between each mark. Work your way round them again deepening them and adjusting any that are off centre. Continue until the grooves are half way down the setting and the claws fully formed. Finish off by filing the bottom of the groove at an angle as shown in Fig. 5-3. Next, working on the bottom of the setting with the three cornered file, divide it up as shown in the same illustration.

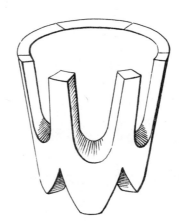

Fig 5.3 Finish off each collet groove by filing the bottom at an angle sloping downwards towards the outside.

Making the Back Bezel

The back bezel is the next item to make. Assuming that you are using the common combination of 18ct white gold for the setting and 18ct yellow gold for the back bezel and shank, you will need a piece of 18ct yellow gold tube whose outside diameter matches the base of the setting. True up one end of the tube and cut off 2 mm. If you have no tube of the right size, a bezel will have to be made from a piece of strip using hard solder for the join. Tap the bezel into a suitable hole in the collet plate or draw plate to give it a taper matching the setting, then file the wide end flat so that the setting rests on it with all the claw bases touching.

To solder the two together grip them lightly in a fine pointed pair of tweezers. Heavy ones will deflect the flame and soak up the heat, making it difficult to solder (Fig. 5-4). Bend the ends of the tweezers if necessary so that they are parallel when holding the two together, if they grip on one side only the bezel and setting may move out of alignment when heated. When one claw base has been

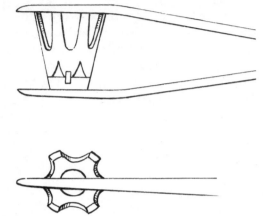

Fig 5.4 Fine tweezers with the ends bent to hold a collet while soldering. Heavy ones will draw away the heat.

soldered to the bezel and the two are still in alignment, change the position of the tweezers and hold the setting by one claw tip so that the tweezers will not interfere with the soldering of the other five. Next solder the base opposite the one you have just soldered so that there is no chance of the first one melting again and the bezel moving out of alignment. The two should be firmly secured now and the remainder can be soldered at will. Use a medium grade of white gold solder for this job as it is easier to clean any stray white solder from the bezel than to remove yellow gold solder from between the claws. If you have no medium grade, easy will do because the easy yellow solder that will be used to solder the setting to the shank is of a lower melting point than white easy.

To make the knife-edge shoulders shown in Fig. 5-5 select a piece of shank wire and cut it 4mm longer than is needed for the finger size. For instance 2 5/16 in or 59 mm will make a ring size N. Instead of cutting a piece out to allow for the setting, leave it the full length. Flux the ends of the shank wire for 5 mm either end. Hold one end in the flame with the curved side towards the flame and the blue inner cone of the flame just touching the end of the

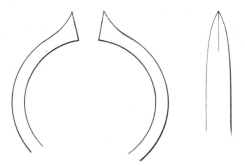

Fig 5.5 Knife edge shoulders seen from the front and side.

wire. Keep the tip of another pair of tweezers just below the end ready to support it if it begins to bend (Fig. 5-6). Keep the end of the wire in the flame until it melts into a ball and begins to roll back. Then take it out of the flame and do the same to the other end. This will give you sufficient metal to hammer up into a point.

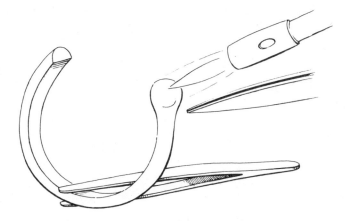

Fig 5.6 Heat the ends of the shank wire to form a blob on each, which can be hammered into a knife edge.

After pickling, bend the wire into a ring with the ends about 5 mm apart and place them on the edge of a flat steel block and hammer the outer edges as thin as possible to form a tapered end as shown in Fig. 5-7. Trim the ends up by sawing where the dotted

*Fig 5.7 Hammering is
done on a steel block.
The shank wire is seen
here from the end.*

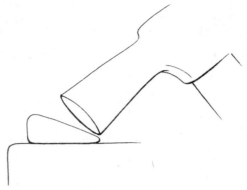

lines indicate in Fig. 5-8 so that the included angle will take the
setting. Finish off by filing the sides flat and bringing them to an
even matching taper. Then emery them smooth. File the underside with the half round file to form a perfect circle. Bring the top
edges to a point and make the curve of both ends match, using the
shallow half of the double half round needle file. All the filing and
emerying on the shoulders should be completed before the setting
is soldered into place because it is more difficult to do it
afterwards.

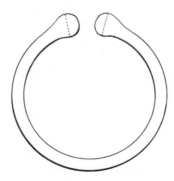

*Fig 5.8 After hammering to a taper, the ends will still be rounded, as seen
here from the sides. Saw off the ends as shown by the dotted lines.*

A small flat is filed on the back bezel and up the claw on opposite
sides of the setting to fit against the ends of the shank. The faces of
the shoulder and the flats of the setting are fluxed and the setting

placed in position with the bottom of the back bezel just clearing the bottom of the shoulders and the claws level and central with the point of each shoulder.

If it looks as if the back bezel is going to be too deep even when the curve to match the ring has been filed into it, pull the shoulders apart a fraction so that the setting drops a little. When everything looks just right and the setting is a gentle friction fit between the shoulders, place a small panel of easy solder between the point of one shoulder and the adjacent claw. This piece is not intended to solder the whole join but just to tack the setting into position so that any final adjustments can be made before the joins are completely soldered. The point of the shoulder and the top of the claw are the thinnest part of the two items so they will get hot first. The solder will run between them before expansion can cause the setting to move.

Look at the setting from top and bottom and both sides. If it lines up centrally with the shoulder, solder the tip of the opposite shoulder and check again. If everything is still nicely lined up, turn the ring upside down and place a panel of solder between the base of one shoulder and the back bezel. With the flame at right angles to the ring so that it concentrates on the join, run the solder into the join and do the same the other side. If, before soldering the back bezel the setting has moved a little and it cannot be bent back into position, cut through one of the joins with the fine saw blade, make the adjustment and resolder.

After pickling the ring, make sure that all the joins have soldered properly and resolder any that have not. Next file away the surplus from the back bezel until it matches the curve of the ring. Put the ring on the triblet, round it up and check the size. If it is oversize, remove a piece from the back of the shank as in a normal sizing job or stretch or enlarge it if it is undersize.

When all the filing and emerying is complete, cut a step into the top of each claw with a round burr in the pendant drill to form a seat for the stone. If there are any file marks in the curve between the claws remove these with a piece of emery paper folded double or wrap it round the tip of the rat-tail file.

All that is left is to polish the ring, allowing the bristle brush plenty of time to polish between the claws. Before setting the stone, clean the inside of the setting as brightly as possible so that all light is reflected back to the stone and not absorbed by dull surfaces.

Making Shoulders

To make a split shoulder with a tube insert, it is not necessary to melt the end of the shank until it rolls back as previously explained. Flux the top 5 mm of the inside of the shank and heat it until it just becomes convex. This prevents it folding over when hammered and forming a groove on the inside as shown in Fig. 5-9.

Hammer the ends just sufficiently to form a flat on either side then make a saw cut as shown in Fig. 5-10 so that the bottom half will be the same thickness as the back bezel when finished. Open up the saw cut with the knife blade until the V gap is wide enough to take the diameter of a small length of tube (Fig. 5-11). When the ends have been shaped and matched, solder the tube in position with a little surplus sticking out each side. If it is not done the solder may melt while the setting is being soldered and flow over the edge and into the tube, blocking it up.

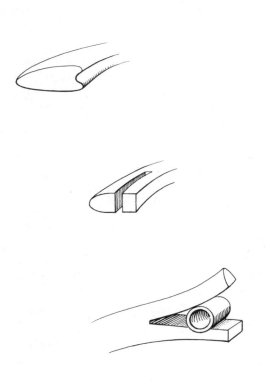

Fig 5.9 (Top, left) If the shank is to have a split shoulder with a tube insert, it is not necessary to form balls on the ends, as with the knife edge shank. Instead, heat the inside ends until they become slightly convex. This will prevent the condition shown above, where subsequent hammering has caused a groove to form.

Fig 5.10 (Top, right) Flatten each end by hammering and make a saw cut as shown.

Fig 5.11 (Below, left) When soldering in the tube after opening the slit with a knife blade, leave a little spare each end to avoid solder running into the tube.

When making the tube shoulders with separate tops it is not necessary to melt or flatten the ends of the shank. Just file away the curved top until what is left will match the thickness of the back bezel. Solder the top of the shoulder by flushing a piece of hard solder into the angle then, holding the shoulder piece in the tweezers at the correct angle to take the tube, reheat the solder. From then on, the procedure is the same as before.

Oval settings can be made by hammering a round cylinder into the oval collet plate. If a round collet plate is all you have, then squash a round setting into an oval shape by gripping in the pliers as shown in Fig. 5-12. Oval stones do not always come in the proportions to fit the oval collet plate. Some are only slightly oval while other are very elongated ovals, so the plate is of fairly limited use.

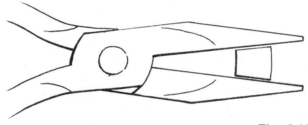

Fig 5.12 Turning a round collet into an oval one with pliers.

The oval setting can be converted into a claw setting in the same way as the round ones just described, but in the larger sizes, about 10 mm by 8 mm, or even smaller if you have the patience. The back bezel need not be a separate piece: the spaces between the feet of the claws can be made by drilling and shaping with the fine piercing saw.

The knife edge shank is not strong enough for these larger stones. The split shank is stronger, more in proportion and simpler to make. A piece of shank wire of sufficient length to give the right size is cut 4 mm longer. This is laid flat on the saw peg and split with the saw (Fig. 5-13) for a distance of about 5 mm. The ends are parted with a knife until one tip of the round nosed pliers will fit between them and they are bent outwards in an even curve. The shank is then bent up into a circle and the ends filed until they match the curve of the setting. With the setting resting evenly bet- ween the four points, one of them is soldered to it. Check the whole thing for alignment, bending where necessary to make corrections. The diagonally opposite tip is soldered next, and then the other two.

The shoulders are usually finished off by filing a double groove at the base of the Y with the three cornered file, then by rounding all the edges as shown in Fig. 5-14. A central piece can be added for strength or decoration or both, or a hollow bead or small setting can be soldered in the triangle.

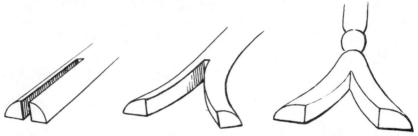

Fig 5.13 A split shank is stronger than a knife edge for larger stones. The ends should be curved outwards with a pair of round-nosed pliers.

Fig 5.14 (Right) A bead is usually formed at the base of the Y for decoration.

For very large stones, it is not easy to make a bezel from strip because, to avoid its looking excessively bulky, the setting has to follow closely the contours of the stone. In these cases it is usually best to make a cage setting from round or flattened wire. See Fig. 5-15. The back bezel should be made sufficiently deep to enable the

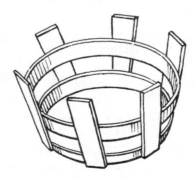

Fig 5.15 A cage setting for very large stones, made to follow the contours of the stone.

inside curve of the ring to be filed out and still leave a reasonable thickness of metal, but the filing of this curve is left until all the soldering has been completed. The join in the back bezel should be soldered with the hard grade of solder and be in the centre of one of the narrow ends of the oval so it is as far away as possible from any subsequent soldering. This enables the claws to be soldered to it with hard solder also, ensuring that it will remain stable while the remainder of the soldering is done.

With a four claw setting, it is possible to solder the claws to the back bezel while holding them in the tweezers because the soldered joins are sufficiently far apart, but with a six claw setting you may, after soldering four in position, have to resort to pressing them into a piece of cuttle fish to keep them in position while the other two are soldered.

With the claws soldered, the next step is to bend them into place so that the stone rests between them with sufficient claw above the girdle to bend over and form the tips. When they are just right, the second bezel is made to fit between the claws and form a seat for the stone. When soldered, it also binds the claws together. When the stone is resting on this, the culet or point at the back of the stone, should just clear the finger.

An octagonal setting, usually a rectangle with the corners off, is made in the same way but, if the stone does not conform to the shapes in the octagonal collet plate, it is an extremely painstaking job to make the two bezels so that they match properly. If the stone does match the collet plate, it is just a matter of forming the bezels roughly into shape and completing them by forcing them into the plate with the punch.

The gallery strip illustrated in Fig. 5-16 is a useful aid to making settings of irregular shape. It is a continuous strip of claws attached to a plain strip which forms the back bezel. The latter is not deep enough to form ring settings of the larger size though it can be deepened to take the curve of the ring by soldering an additional strip to it.

Fig 5.16 Gallery strip, available ready-made from material dealers.

Very small four claw settings can be bought ready-made in various materials which are handy for fitting into the triangle of the split shank if shoulder stones are required. Alternatively a short length of tube can be used with four claws formed into it with the file.

Star Settings

Sometimes one is asked to fit a stone into a wedding ring or in the table of a signet ring in a way that it will not protrude above the surface. A star setting (Fig. 5-17) is used for this purpose and though it comes within the realm of the specialist setter, it is not beyond the capabilities of a jeweller, using care and some practise beforehand.

Fig 5.17 A star setting, used when a small stone is to be set flush with the surface, as in some signet rings.

The first step is to mark where the centre of the stone is to be and drill a pilot hole. This is enlarged to about half the diameter of the stone or a little more if it will not weaken the ring too much at that point. Next a burr is used to enlarge the front of the hole to take the stone. The job can be made relatively easy if the stone is a tight fit in the hole. If it is loose, it will move about while you are trying to set it. In this case, there is more chance of the graver slipping and breaking off the grains you are trying to push over the stone. Also, the grains have to be large enough to bridge any gap between the sides of the hole and the stone, which makes them doubly difficult to raise from the surface.

The hole should be deep enough so that there is a rim of metal above the girdle of the stone when it is in place. Mark the position of the four arms of the star 90 degrees apart and, using a narrow, round-bottomed graver, dig it into the metal a small fraction from the stone at each of the four positions to form the beginnings of a grain. Do not try to push them over the stone or the stone may tilt and the grain break off. If the stone was a tight fit to begin with, it should be firmly held at this point and you can work your way round the grains again digging a little deeper and forcing the grains over the edge of the stone by levering the graver over as shown in Fig. 5-18.

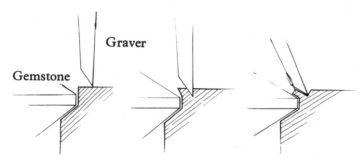

Fig 5.18 Using a graver to form one of the grains to hold the stone.

When a look through the eyeglass tells you the stone is firmly held and the grains are over the edge of the stone, it is time to begin forming the star. The square graver is used for the next part. It should be sharpened as shown in Fig. 5-19 and the three 'cutting' surfaces polished by stroking them on a piece of polishing paper laid on a flat hard surface. Stroke away from the point all the time, or the graver may dig in and the cutting edge become dulled. The sharper it is, the less chance of your slipping and cutting off the grains. A test for sharpness that engravers use is to tap the point lightly against the thumb nail. If it sticks, it is sharp; if it slips, it isn't.

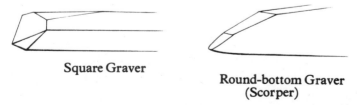

Fig 5.19 (Left) How a square graver should be sharpened for cutting the star.

From the point of each arm of the star, cut a fine line, stopping just short of the grain. Then flick the tip of the graver out of the metal so that the shaving that has formed is broken off. Fig.5-20

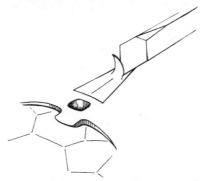

Fig 5.20 The start of a star cut, which should be very fine and made with very little effort.

shows the start of the cut. The first cut should be so fine that very little effort is required to move the graver and you have full control of it. If the thumbs are pressed together as shown in Fig. 5-21, there

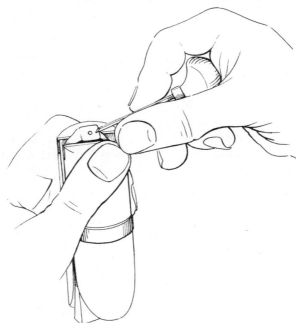

Fig 5.21 With the ring in a ring clamp and the thumbs pressed together as shown, there should be little chance of the graver slipping.

should be in no danger of slipping. Repeat the process beginning a little further from the point of the star with each cut and stop when the cut is about the same depth as the base of the grain. The arms of the star will not be wide enough yet, but you will have built up a small wall in front of the grain which should prevent you chopping it off when using the chisel edge graver to widen them.

Chisel Edge Graver

The chisel edge graver should have its two cutting surfaces polished. The shine is transferred to the metal you are cutting and the brighter it is the better. Place one corner of the graver in the bottom of the groove already cut and take a slice off one side of the groove, cutting a little deeper the nearer you get to the stone (Fig. 5-22). Do the same to the other side of the groove then repeat on

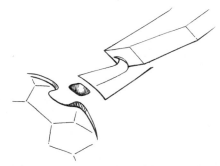

Fig 5.22 Cutting a star facet with a chisel edged graver. The bright finish should come from the brightly polished end of the graver.

the other three arms, keeping them an even width. It is better to do a little bit often rather than try to reach the whole width in one stroke. When the star is looking like the diagram Fig. 5-23, it is time to cut away the wall in front of the grain. Using one corner of the chisel edge graver, cut down towards the centre of the arm and away from the grain. Then repeat on the other side of the arm until the wall is removed and the cuts match up to the two sides of the arm.

To form the shorter arms of the star, scribe a short line to mark their centres equidistant between the long arms. Place the corner of the chisel edge graver at the base of one arm as shown in Fig. 5-24 and cut down at an angle towards the centre line; then do the

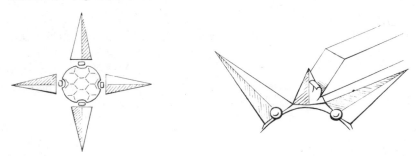

Fig 5.23 (Left) The main cuts of the star are formed here except for the outer ends nearest the stone, i.e. the wall in front of the grain, which should now be cut away. The finished main cuts can be seen in Fig 5.17.

Fig 5.24 (Right) Forming the shorter arms of the star with a chisel edged graver. Here the grains are shown rounded, normally a last operation.

same from the other side so that you remove a small triangle of metal with a distinct angle where the centre line was. Do the same between the other three arms and go over them again lightly if they do not match.

The secret of success lies in having very sharp, well polished gravers with the angles just right. If they are too acute, the points break off easily; if too obtuse, too much pressure is needed and they slip. Practice on a piece of copper sheet with some synthetic spinels and after half a dozen tries you will begin to get the feel of things. It is one of those skills you can only acquire with practice.

Finally, using a suitable graining tool, round off the grains and burnish them down on to the stone at the same time by twisting and rolling the tool in one motion as shown in Fig. 5-25.

Fig 5.25 The graining tool should be twisted and rocked in one motion to round and polish the grains.

A very simple setting can be made for small round cabochon cut stones from a plain round disc. The disc should be about a third larger in diameter than the stone. Place the stone in the centre of the disc and scribe a line round it. Grip it anywhere on the circumference with the round nosed pliers so that the tip of the pliers is level with the scribed line and bend the rim upwards as shown in Fig. 5-26. Move the pliers to a point directly opposite the first and bend upwards again. Do this again in the centre of the two remaining flat parts so that you have what amounts to four claws. Fit the stone in the centre and force them over the stone with the sharp edge of the tweezers.

Fig 5.26 Bending up the edge of a disc in four places to form a simple setting for a cabochon-cut stone.

The disc has to be fairly thin for the folds to be sharp, for a 4 mm diameter stone not more than 0.012 inch (0.3mm) thick. The method makes ideal ear studs as well as sitting nicely on a split shank with the ends soldered together (Fig. 5-27).

Fig 5.27 The complete setting with a stone. It is also useful for making ear studs.

Half Eternity Rings

Making a half eternity ring might seem a bit daunting to the beginner but, if taken step by step, it is much easier than making a claw-setting.

For a platinum setting on a yellow gold shank, select a piece of square wire about 1 mm wider than the diameter of the stones. Square wire straight from the rolls will have blunt corners, so you will need a slightly thicker piece which you can pass through the sheet rollers a few times to sharpen the corners.

Cut off 2½ in (6.5 cm), more or less depending on the size of the finished ring, and mark the centre, i.e. 1¼ in (3.25 cm) from one end. This will coincide with the centre of your centre stone. With the spring dividers mark a line each side of this where the edges of the stone will be. Allow space between each stone. This will vary depending on the size of the stone, 1 mm is about right for a 0.1 carat diamond. Mark out the positions of the remaining six stones, assuming it to be a seven-stone ring. Scribe a deep line 0.5 mm clear of each end stone then clamp the wire in a half round groove on the rollers and form the shank by rolling from each end up to this mark or as near as you can judge. Next soften the wire and bend it into the ring, join it and round it up.

Cut a piece of platinum strip for the setting just slightly wider than the square part of the ring and about 0.5 mm thick and bend it so that it matches the curve of the ring perfectly. File the top of the ring where the setting is to go so that the two fit together with no gaps. Flux them both and bind them together with iron binding wire, a couple of turns at each end and one in the middle (Fig 5-28).

Fig 5.28 Making a platinum setting for several small stones on a gold shank.

Place two panels of easy yellow solder as shown in the same illustration. Easy can be used because this will be the only soldered join. Heat the ring from the inside so that the solder will not be tempted to run over the platinum top. When it has vanished into the join, see if it has run through to the other side and each end. If not, put small panels of solder on the unsoldered spots and heat again. When it is completely soldered, remove the iron wire and pickle the ring.

Never put iron or steel into the pickle as it will contaminate it and any silver articles put in it afterwards will come out bright red. Stainless steel tweezers will not affect it, if dipped in momentarily.

When the ring is pickled and dry, file away the surplus setting from the edges. Mark where the centre of the centre stone will be and drill a pilot hole here. Widen it to half the diameter of the stone

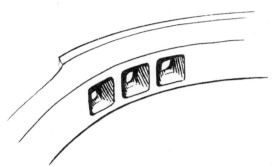

Fig 5.29 The holes at the back of the setting should be squared off to provide a professional finish.

and widen the top with a burr until the stone is a perfect fit. Once you have established the distance between the centres of two adjacent stones, set the points of the spring dividers that far apart and mark the centres of each stone. Drill the pilot holes. Be very careful to get the holes equally spaced because, although it is possible to disguise inaccuracies on the setting, it is very obvious when looked at from the back. Chamfer the back of the holes with a large burr. For a professional-looking finish, these holes at the back can be squared off with a square graver or square file. It is a fiddly job, but well worth the effort (Fig. 5-29).

When all the settings have been drilled to take the stones, file and emery the ring and give it a preliminary polish.

Next, press the centre stone into its setting. If it is a tight fit, it makes the job of digging out the grains that much easier. As with the star-setting, dig the round bottom graver into the metal 0.25 mm to 0.5 mm from the edge of the stone in the positions shown in Fig. 5-30, then work your way round again, levering the grains forward a little each time.

When all the stones are in place, use the square graver to make cuts in the setting where the dotted lines are in the diagram (Fig. 5-31). Make shallow cuts first so that you have full control of the graver, then gradually deepen them.

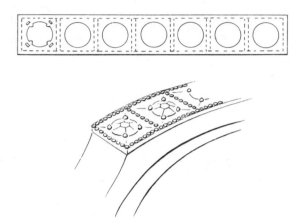

Fig 5.30 (Top) The grains to hold the stones are positioned where shown on the left. However, it is best to start setting with the centre stone. After the stones are set, make shallow grooves with the graver where the dotted lines are above, deepen them and then use a suitable milligrain tool to raise the beading.

Fig 5.31 (Above) The finished setting should look something like this.

Next, go over the raised edges and the ridge you have formed between each stone with a suitable size millgraining tool. Also with a graining tool, round off and burnish all the grains on to the stones.

The final job is to remove the bareness from the shelf surrounding the stones. This has to be levelled with the chisel graver, working from the grain towards the centre in each case, to avoid cutting off the grain. If the graver is sharp and highly polished, very little effort will be needed. Bevel it off until the inner edge is almost level with the stone, as in Fig. 5-31.

Polish again, using the bristle brush on the setting with just the lightest touch on the mop to finish off. Too long on the mop and the sharpness will be taken off the setting so that it will lose its sparkle.

Chapter 6

Wristware

Gold wristwatches, often with gold bracelets, are a fairly regular feature in repair work. Often they are prized possessions received on a birthday or as a wedding present and people tend to keep them even when they are badly worn.

The expanding watch bracelet illustrated in Fig. 6-1 is usually in this category. Happily they are becoming extinct, but they still keep turning up for repairing and respringing. One complete link

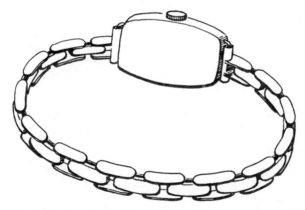

Fig 6.1 An old type of watch bracelet no longer made, which sometimes turns up for repair as it is someone's prized possession.

consists of a hollow centre link containing two springs, and two side links joined together by two bars, called runners, which compress the springs when the bracelet is expanded. (See Fig. 6-2).

The springs become slack with age; also wear on the runners and centre link allows the springs to jump over the runners so that the bracelet will not contract fully when on the wrist.

Fig 6.2 *The centre link, which has two springs, shown with one of the two side links.*

If one comes to you for respringing only, it is best to check for wear before attempting any respringing. The links nearest to the watch tend to wear first, so check the runners and centre links for wear at the points indicated in Fig. 6-3 and, if it is excessive, return it with a quote for strengthening as well as respringing, otherwise you may find it back on your bench in a few weeks' time with the words: 'Just been done' on the packet. You will find yourself having to strengthen it for nothing to keep the bracelet and your reputation intact.

If the wear is only slight, the bracelet can safely be resprung. First remove all the old springs with a fine pointed pair of tweezers, then polish and clean it. Make sure it is thoroughly dry before putting any new springs in it or they will rust. Close any centre links that have opened up until the runners are just free to move. Pressing them together with the tweezers will close the gap.

Wear on runners

Wear on centre link

Fig 6.3 *Places where the centre and side links tend to wear.*

Springs are sold in packets containing a 12 in (30 cm) length. The size is stamped on the packet and it is as well to keep a range in stock as they are cheap. The most useful sizes are: 1.5, 2, 2.5 and 3.

Select a spring that will fill the cavity in the centre link but be free to move. If you use a spring that is too small, it will soon work its way over the runner. With the tweezers, bend in the end of the spring towards the centre as shown in Fig. 6-4. Then level the first coil up so that it presents a flat face to the runner. Press the first coil into the centre link then screw it in until it fills just over half of the link (Fig. 6-5). Compress it with the side link and check that it will not jump over the runner and that it fully expands again when released. If it is correct, snip off the spring as close as possible to where it enters the centre link and tuck the end in with the tweezers. This is repeated right the way through the bracelet until

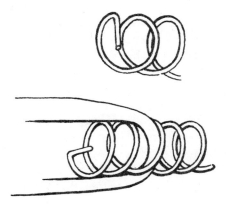

Fig 6.4 (Top) Bending the end of a spring towards the centre makes it easier to fit.
Fig 6.5 Screw in the spring until it fills just over half the centre link, position it as explained in the text, and cut off the spare end.

it is completely resprung. Do not put too much spring in the links or it will force its way over the runner. Put an equal amount in each side or too much strain will be placed on the shorter spring and again it will be forced over the runner.

A variation of this type of link has a central wire running the length of the centre link which passes through a hole in the runners. This prevents the springs getting over the runners. It is fixed at each end and the spring is wound around it. There is a small hole in the end of the centre link and a new spring is fitted by inserting the end through the hole and screwing it on to the wire.

Sometimes worn runners can be strengthened by running a spot of solder into the worn cavity (see Fig. 6-3). If, however, only a very fine piece of metal is holding it together, the solder will not be drawn into the cavity and often the thread of metal remaining melts before the solder. In this case the runner has to be replaced.

If you have to replace both runners on one pair of side links, do them one at a time. It is far easier to wedge a new one into place, solder it and then cut out the other and replace that, than it is to cut them both out at the same time. It is difficult to position two new ones, get them the same length and identical, solder them and finish up with everything in alignment. If you get one where the side links have broken apart, replace one runner first by soldering it to the two side links. Line them up, then wedge the other runner between them and solder that. Do not try to solder two runners to one side link, then the other side link to the ends of the runners. It is possible, but it makes an easy job difficult.

Wear on the centre link (Fig. 6-3) cannot be dealt with satisfactorily. You can slow down the wearing process by smoothing the worn edges as much as possible and pressing the halves closer together. The runner will then have as little free movement in the slot as possible. You may have to fit slightly smaller springs in the links treated in this way.

If a link has to be removed or added, a centre link will have to be opened up in order to do so. There is a soldered join at one end of every centre link, which can be opened by fluxing it and gently heating it while lightly levering it apart with two pair of tweezers. If the solder is reluctant to melt, do not risk melting the link. Cut the join open with a 4/0 saw blade. It is better to melt it apart if you can, because the small amount of metal removed by the saw blade can result in the slot becoming tapered, causing the runners to stick.

There is a less common type of bracelet where the centre links have no join. On these the side links are hollow and have a slot running down the centre on the inside. In the middle of the link the slot opens out into a circle. Instead of being soldered, the runners have round discs at each end, like pin heads, which fit into the circle and are then slid along into position at the end as in Fig. 6-6. This type is often combined with the guide wire running down the centre link. To add or remove a link, it is only necessary to slide the runner along the slot until it reaches the circle then lift it out. Sometimes a fine curved leaf spring is fitted loose in the hollow side link to prevent the runner accidentally moving along the slot and coming apart. Compress this with a needle point while you ease the foot of the runner back over it.

A common type of watch bracelet that comes in for repair is the snake bracelet, so named because of its appearance and flexibility. It can be either a single strand or two strand but in either case the strands terminate at both ends in a cup which is a one-piece press-

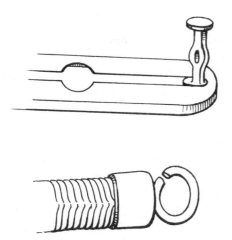

Fig 6.6 (Top) Another type of spring link watch bracelet with removable runners.

Fig 6.7 The end of a snake bracelet, where it tends to wear and break. The bracelet will have to be detached from the watch and the broken piece removed from the cup end by heat or grinding.

ing into which the ends are pushed then soldered (Fig. 6-7). These bracelets tend to wear and break where the snake chain enters the cup at the watch end. The cup is attached to the watch by either a tube hinge or a large ring. In either case it is necessary to detach it from the watch before any repair can be carried out.

The broken end of the chain can usually be removed from the cup by fluxing and heating it and pulling it out with a pair of tweezers while the cup is gripped in another pair. If the end was a tight fit before it was soldered, you may have to grind some of it out with a dental burr before it can be removed with the tweezers.

Once the new end has been made to fit the cup it is best to heat, pickle and clean it with wire wool before trying to solder it. This type of chain becomes filled with dirt and grease which is not apparent from the outside, but as soon as the chain is heated, the dirt boils out in a black 'goo' and makes it impossible to solder. When cleaning it with wire wool, clean only the part that will be inside the cup because the solder has the tendency to run along the chain and make it solid. If the oxide is left, it discourages the solder. For this reason it is best, if the chain is not broken through, to cut it and reterminate it rather than butt solder the frayed pieces. If you try, inevitably you end up with a stiff section of chain which reduces the flexibility and accelerates wear.

Repairing the bracelet in this way shortens it by a fraction, but most are fitted with adjustable ladder snaps which can compensate for this.

Bracelet Attachment

There are three principle ways in which jewellery style watch bracelets are attached to watches: the tube joints, the cocktail loop and the lug or goalpost (see Fig. 6-8). These are all main points of wear. With the tube joint it is usually necessary to replace the three tubes and the rivet joining them together. With the cocktail loop it is easier and makes a longer-lasting repair if you enlarge the loop a little and insert a small section of thick walled tube rather than try to butt solder a piece where the worn part was. The lugs, being just a piece of bent wire, are easy to replace. If the halves of the watch case are hinged together, however, the hinge is usually next to the feet of the lugs, so take the rivet out of the hinge and remove the back before trying to fit new lugs or the hinge will probably solder solid. If the rivet is difficult to remove, burnish the tubes a little to enlarge them and make sure you are pushing the small end of the tapered pin.

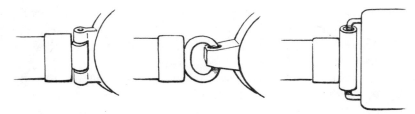

Fig 6.8 Three ways in which jewellery style bracelets are attached to watches.

In each of these cases, it goes without saying that the movement and glass are removed before any soldering is carried out. If the case is not hinged, the halves usually clip together and if no work is to be done on the back, the back can be removed and the movement left in it for safety.

If the movement has to be taken out, check whether or not it is working first, and if it is not, *make a note on the packet.* It often happens that when the bracelet breaks the watch falls to the floor but the only damage the owner sees is the broken bracelet. The overlooked broken balance staff might be blamed on you when the customer gets his watch back and finds it is not working.

Older-type watch cases are often of three-piece construction, a front containing the glass, the body holding the movement and a removable back. In these, the watch movement lifts out of the body from the front but is held in position by two case screws and the winding button. The case screws usually have to be removed and can be recognised by their large heads and the fact that a section of the head overlaps the edge of the case as shown in Fig. 6-9. Sometimes the case screw has only half a head, so that it need only be given a half turn to free it. The small screw right next to the winding button is the one holding it in place. Do not remove it entirely. Usually one or two turns are all that is necessary before the button can be lifted out. If you remove this screw completely, the piece that it was screwed into drops out of place and is very difficult to get back.

Always store movements in a transparent plastic box when they are out of the case so that you can see them. Then you will not forget which box they are in and inadvertantly rattle the contents to find out if the box is empty. Always handle the movement by the edges or, if possible, the button. Your fingers always leave traces of perspiration and the shining steel parts rust easily. Some watchmakers handle valuable movements in tissue paper.

A repair that often has to be carried out on square or octagonal gold watch cases is filling holes that have worn at the corners on the front of the case (see Fig. 6-10). Sometimes when they are only pinholes, you may find that they have been plugged with soft (lead) solder. This quickly wears away as the hole gets bigger but always

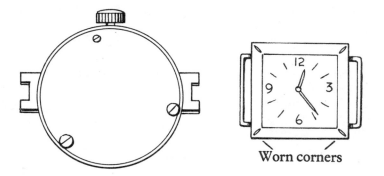

Worn corners

Fig 6.9 (Left) Case screws holding a watch movement in place can be rocognised by their larger heads overlapping the edge of the case.
Fig 6.10 The corners wear on square and some other shaped watches. Such pinholes are sometimes filled with soft solder which will have to be removed before repairing them correctly with gold solder.

leaves traces on the inside. Any soft solder will have to be removed completely before any gold soldering can be carried out.

If the case is heated gently until the soft solder is just beginning to melt, it can be brushed out with a stiff bristled paint brush. This will get rid of the bulk of the solder. The remaining traces can be scraped away with a chisel graver or wire brush in the pendant drill. One sure way of getting rid of it all is to immerse the case in hydrochloric acid for an hour or two. This will dissolve it. If there is the slightest trace of lead left on the case, it will burn into the gold when heated and make a hole or brittle patch that will drop out at a touch.

To repair the hole, it is best to file it on the front until the edges are broad and flat, then solder a patch over the hole. When it has been pickled and cleaned, file away the surplus edge of the patch until no evidence of it can be seen. Very small holes can be patched from the inside, but if they are much more than a crack, the solder will not be drawn into them. Although the case may then be dust-proof, the shape of the hole will still be visible.

One oddment that may come your way is the silver marcasite watch bracelet. These usually consist of links 10 mm to 15 mm (.4-.6 in), long joined together with a bar and loop as in Fig. 6-11. When the bars wear, the links are usually thick enough to be drilled through as shown and a new bar riveted or soft soldered in place. Marcasites will not stand the heat of hard soldering. When the loop wears, the hole can usually be rounded up and a small section of silver tube soft soldered in, as in Fig. 6-12. Do not put

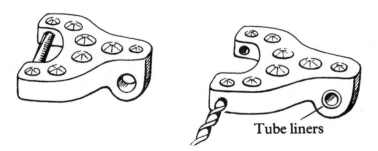

Tube liners

Fig 6.11 (Left) The usual type of link of a silver and marcasite watch bracelet.

Fig 6.12 (Right) Worn link holes of silver and marcasite watch bracelets should be bushed with silver tube.

marcasite jewellery in the ultrasonic cleaner, the violence of the action will shake a great many of the stones out and although it may be a good test of their security, you will not get paid for replacing them.

Many modern wrist watches have integral bracelets, usually of very close meshed links joined together on the gate bracelet principle. If one of these comes to you for shortening, before you attempt the difficult task of removing the runner, examine the edges of the bracelet near the fastener. Often the first three or four links each side of the fastener are held in place by a long screw instead of a runner, which makes shortening it a very simple task. Usually only a series of round holes is visible on the edge, as the screw head is deeply recessed. Such a screw can be reached, however, with a watchmaker's screwdriver.

Gold Watch Cases

Gold and rolled gold watch cases are sometimes fitted with spring-loaded bars for attaching the bracelet. One of these consist of a section of steel tube containing a coil spring. A moveable plug is fitted to each end of the tube. The ends of these are narrower and fit into a matching hole in the lugs of the watch case (Fig. 6-13). A spring lug is slotted into a tube on each end of the watch bracelet and compressed until it slides between the lugs of the case. When the narrow ends are opposite the holes in the lugs, the bar expands forcing the ends into position and securing the bracelet.

The holes into which the spring bar ends fit, tend to wear towards the back of the case until they finally break through. To rebuild them, use a piece of gold tube that the bar ends will just fit into, then enlarge the original hole in the case to take the outside diameter of the tube. Solder a short length of tube into each hole and fill the gap between the tube and the back of the case with solder as in Fig. 6-14.

The original hole may have been blind, i.e. did not go completely through the lug. It is best, if it will not disfigure or weaken the case, to drill the hole right through, or the solder may flow into the gap between the tube and the case. It will then fill the tube, making it solid. Drilling the holes right through also makes it easier to remove the spring bars by merely pressing a pin into the hole. When removing a spring bar, always be ready to catch it when it is free of the arm. The springs are quite powerful and the lug will shoot off like a bullet if you are not prepared for it.

Fig 6.13 A spring-loaded bar fitted into blind holes in a watch lug. It passes through a loop in the strap to attach the strap. The holes become worn to one side.

Fig 6.14 (Far right) A worn lug hole will have to be drilled larger and round, from the outside. If it is blind and not right throught the lug, the starting point for the drill will have to be estimated. It is then bushed with the appropriate size tube and lastly the gap remaining outside the tube should be filled with solder.

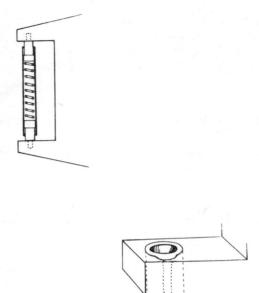

On some gold watch cases, the lugs are a one-piece pressing soldered on to the case as shown in Fig. 6-15. These become worn at the points shown by the dotted line and cannot usually be built up with solder. It is a long and costly job to cut out two complete lugs. The usual remedy is to replace the bar only. If the new one is a

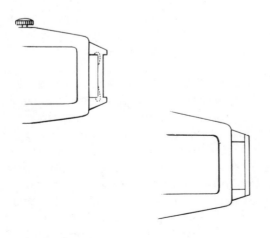

Fig 6.15 (Far left) Some gold cases have integral lugs on the same principle as illustrated here, which wear as shown by the dotted lines.

Fig 6.16 The wear shown in Fig 6.15 cannot usually be repaired by solder filling. The easiest remedy is to cut off the bar and solder on a new one.

gentle push fit between the lugs, it can usually be soldered with easy solder without disturbing the join between the lug and the case. Sometimes the edge of the bracelet has worn into the lug as well, in which case it is easier to remove the tips of the lugs as well as the bar and solder a new bar across the ends of the arms as shown also in Fig. 6-16.

Hollow bangles have three common faults: dents, worn hinges and faulty or broken snaps. Dents can be removed by soldering the end of a piece of wire to the centre of the dent and pulling it out. Hold the bangle in the left hand and use the top of the thumb as a lever for the pliers in the right hand, so that the pull is controlled and the dent not turned into a hump (Fig. 6-17). Sometimes the dent pops out perfectly, but more often than not, the wire will have

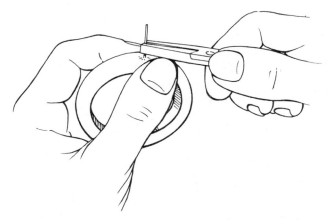

Fig 6.17 A dent in a hollow bracelet can be pulled out by soldering on a length of wire and using pliers to pull. The pliers should be levered against the thumb to control the pull and avoid turning the dent into a hump.

to be moved to different positions and pulled again and any remaining irregularities filled with solder.

The tubes of the hinge of a hollow bangle are usually soldered to plates that are in turn soldered to the ends of the bangle (Fig. 6-18). For this reason it is very risky to try to heat the tubes and lift them off when they need replacing. The plate is liable to come with them and it is difficult to reposition them. It is safer to saw and file them away. Make sure that you remove all the old solder and use only the minimum amount of easy solder for fitting the new tubes.

Fig 6.18 The hinge of a hollow bangle is usually of this form. If damaged, attempts to unsolder the tubes will probably also loosen the end plates and make repair very difficult. It is better to file away damaged parts and fit new tubes by easy solder.

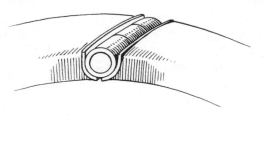

Any excess will run along the plates and prevent the hinge mating properly. Replace the two outside tubes first, then you can cut the middle one and make it an exact fit before soldering it in place. If you use home-made tube with a seam in it, solder the seam with high melting point solder before fitting it to the bangle or you may find the solder being drawn through the seam and into the tube. It will then have to be cleaned out before a rivet can be fitted.

When the new hinge mates satisfactorily, put a broach in it and taper the hole. To make a tapered pin to fit it, put a piece of suitable round wire in the pin vice, file a slight groove in the bench peg and, resting the wire in that, rotate it as you file it. When it is a good fit in the hinge, finish it off with emery paper before finally fitting it in place. It should be a good enough fit to prevent the two parts from flopping about under their own weight. If it is loose, broach out the two outer tubes until the looseness goes. Snip off the surplus pin and file the large end flush with the tube but leave enough on the small end for it to be riveted over with the hammer.

Snap Fastener Wear

The snap fastener usually wears at the points shown in Fig. 6-19. On the male half, this can be compensated for by bending the corners up. On the female half the wear is not visible. The inside edge develops a slope which allows the worn tongue to pull out easily. The slope has to be filed away with a needle file or, if it has worn too much, the plate is replaced. It is not necessary to replace the whole of the plate, which is a long and difficult job. Just file away the top as shown in Fig. 6-20 and replace it by two short strips, or one long one which can be cut apart after soldering.

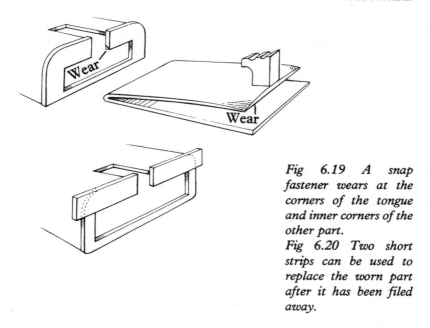

Fig 6.19 A snap fastener wears at the corners of the tongue and inner corners of the other part.

Fig 6.20 Two short strips can be used to replace the worn part after it has been filed away.

If the tongue has lost its springiness, it is usually only necessary to hammer the tip on a block, then open it up again with a penknife. Often the reason the tension has gone is because the tongue is cracked across the tip. In this case, it will have to be broken off, the faces of the crack filed clean and the top soldered back on again. It can be held in position while the soldering is done by placing a piece of wire under it as shown in Fig. 6-21.

If a bangle comes to you with the whole of the tongue missing, it is not a difficult job to make a new one, just a matter of folding over a piece of metal of the right width and thickness and soldering a thumbpiece on to it. The difficult part is soldering it into place without the thumbpiece moving or falling over, even if hard grade solder has been used. The best way of doing it is to cut a slot in the face plate. Wedge the tongue into this and solder it, then put the thumbpiece on afterwards. Quite often the original was fitted in this way, so it is only a matter of cleaning the broken bit out of the slot. Very occasionally the tongue is not soldered in but is a moveable fit in the slot. This has been achieved by making it a double-ended tongue as shown in Fig. 6-22. If you need to remove it, you will have to drill a pinhole into the hollow part so you can compress it with a pin and pull it out.

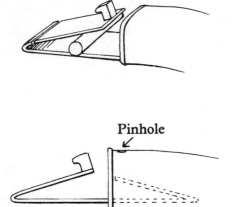

Pinhole

Fig 6.21 (Top) Tongues that have broken off can be resoldered after being cleaned up, using a wire as a support.
Fig 6.22 (Below) To replace a double-ended tongue like this requires a hole to be drilled in the bracelet in order to insert a pin to compress the inner tongue.

If a hollow bangle is badly bent as shown in Fig. 6-23, it will have to be broken through at the bend in order to reshape it. When the halves match up, clean the inside of them for about 5mm and insert either a solid plug or a piece of sheet, bent to fit the inside so that the halves will hold together while being soldered and will be reinforced at that point.

The hollow curb bracelet is one that presents a peculiar difficulty. With age, the solder joining the links deteriorates and the links break apart. It is no use cleaning the join and trying to resolder it, as you would with a solid one, because the solder runs inside the hollow link and will not stay in the join. To overcome this, a thin piece of sheet is inserted in the join and each half of the

Fig 6.23 A hollow bracelet that has been bent has to be repaired by breaking it in two through the bend, reshaped, and resoldered with a plug inside.

link soldered to it and then the excess sheet is snipped and filed away (Fig. 6-24).

When these links wear, there is usually a distinct semi-circle at each end of the link. Each can be built up by soldering a short length of shank wire in the groove (Fig. 6-25). This is then rounded up with a rat-tail needle file until it matches the contours of the link.

If you are as curious as I was as to how hollow tube is twisted into such a shape without kinking, I will give you the explanation I was eventually given. Before bending, the tube is filled with a material called 'Wood's metal' which is an alloy containing 5 parts bismuth, 2 parts tin, 4 parts lead and 2 parts cadmium. It has a melting point of only 71C (160F). The tube can be treated like solid wire when it is filled with this material and, when the links are all bent into shape, they are boiled in water and the Wood's metal melts and runs out.

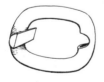

Fig 6.24 Hollow links of a curb bracelet can cause problems. If the link is cut through and reshaped, the ends can be soldered together with a thin sheet of the same metal between them. The surplus is then filed off.

Fig 6.25 (Far left) Worn hollow links can be repaired by soldering a piece of solid shank wire in the worn part and filing it to the correct contour.

Occasionally these bracelets have a padlock fastener that is operated by a small key or, more often, a spring-loaded catch on one side. If the hasp has to be strengthened or a broken spring replaced, you will have to open up the padlock to remove the spring. Sometimes the front is wrongly soft soldered on because the spring would become softened under the heat of hard soldering. On others the imitation screw heads on the front are actually rivet heads that have been cut to look like screws. A close examination will soon tell you which method has been used. With a soft soldered one, it is just a matter of warming it until the solder melts so that part of the padlock can be removed. With the rivet version the heads will have to be filed or drilled away and new rivets fitted.

Solid curb bracelets sometimes need lengthening and if you do not have a suitable link in stock, you will have to make one. Using a piece of wire of matching diameter, bend up an oval link with the round-nosed pliers, making it the same width as the existing curb links but slightly longer. Solder the join, then grip it in two pairs of pliers as shown in Fig. 6-26 and twist the link until it matches the bracelet. If you need several links, make the ovals and solder them together in a chain. Then grip the two end ones and twist as before until all the links are curbed. You may have to give the links a bit of individual attention afterwards to get them to lie properly.

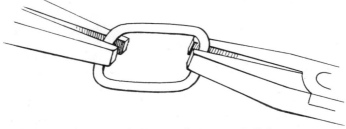

Fig 6.26 Using two pairs of pliers to form a curb link.

Ordinary padlocks often need the hasps replacing. It is easy enough to solder a piece of tube to the end of a piece of wire and bend it into shape, but it is quicker if you make the wire a little overlength and hammer the last 4mm or 5mm flat on the block as shown in Fig. 6-27. Bend that into a tube or loop (Fig. 6-28).

Some curb bracelets are lengths of old watch chain that have been shortened and the swivel that held the watch used as a fastener. If the loop of the swivel needs strengthening, you will have to remove the spring first. If you examine the base of the moveable part, you will find it is held in place by a taper pin. These pins are usually a very good fit and difficult to detect. Once you have found the narrow end of the pin and pressed it out, the moveable part comes away and you can lift out the piece of coil spring.

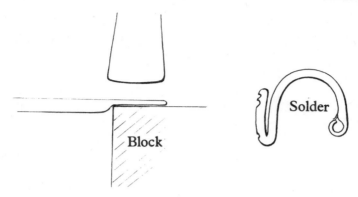

Fig 6.27 (Left) A quick way of making a padlock hasp by flattening what is to be the hinge end of a piece of wire.
Fig 6.28 The flattened end of the wire is bent into a loop. This avoids having to solder on a piece of tube.

Charm Bracelets

There is nothing difficult about soldering a charm to a bracelet. Gold ones can be held in the tweezers, but silver ones usually have to be done on the asbestos block because the tweezers become too hot to hold. The big difficulty lies in the great variety of charms that can be damaged by heat.

On souvenir charms such as miniature Eiffel towers, St. Paul's cathedrals and wedding charms, there is often a tiny plastic micro-lens with an actual photograph of the building or whatever built into it. These will melt and burn if not spotted (Fig. 6-29).

What often appears to be vitreous enamel is paint or lacquer and goes up with a quick flash, usually accompanied by a four-letter word. A dig with a pin will distinguish which is which: vitreous enamel is like glass and will not mark. Dutch charms, usually in the shape of a pair of clogs, have blue windmills on a white background painted on them and look very much like enamel. I well remember carefully removing the imitation cigarettes from a replica packet of Players only to see the 'enamel' go up in a puff of smoke. It took ages to get that bearded sailor looking right again.

Silver charms have two pitfalls peculiar to them. Manufacturers often finish them in a tumble polisher containing minute steel ball bearings. These become jammed at the bottom of toby jugs and in the toes of shoes and such-like places. If their presence is not noticed until the bracelet is pickled, it comes out of the pickle bright pink. The steel reacts with the acid and the copper oxide already dissolved in it and the pink is deposited copper. Usually the only satisfactory way to deal with it is to silver plate over it.

Charms containing old £1 or 10 shilling notes were not such a tragedy if damaged when those notes were in circulation, but they are very difficult to replace today. It is not that one would try to hard solder them, but sometimes a bit of deflected flame strikes the transparent cover. Plastic covers begin to melt and smell and are usually caught in time but some are made of celluloid and burn instantly, leaving you with a perforated note.

Charms of base metal that will not stand the heat of hard soldering should have a stronger ring fitted which is soft soldered. If a bracelet comes in to have just one or two charms soldered, make sure that the charms already on the bracelet have not been soft soldered. If any have, position them so that the solder will not be reheated when the new ones are being soldered.

Gate Bracelets

The common fault with gate bracelets is that the runners become worn or the soldered ends come adrift. The main difficulty with fitting a new runner is to keep it in place while it is being soldered. The best way of doing this is to allow gravity to pull on it. The new runner should be about 2 mm overlength at each end. When it is in position and the bracelet suspended as shown in Fig. 6-30, put the merest touch of flux on the ends and the minimum amount of

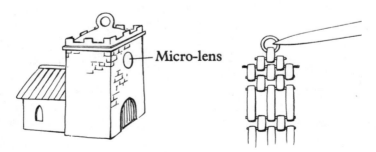

— Micro-lens

Fig 6.29 (Left) Charms for bracelets are sometimes fitted with tiny lenses which will melt and burn if not noticed before applying heat.

Fig 6.30 A method of soldering a new runner in a gate bracelet without the solder running into another joint. The new runner or pivot is overlength to start with and the bracelet is suspended.

solder and heat the extended surplus piece first. All this is to ensure that the solder does not run down the runner and join the next link up as well. The instant the solder runs, take it out of the flame.

Thin Wire Bangles

Thin wire bangles tend to break fairly easily because they have to be distorted slightly in order to get them over the broad part of the hand. Because of this, it is useless to repair them with a straight butt join, they would soon break again. Always use a long lap join. Very large mandrels can be obtained for reshaping these bracelets. They are used in much the same way as you would reshape a ring on the triblet. Unless they are used a lot, however, such mandrels are not worth the outlay. A milk bottle full of sand can be used in its place if you are gentle and accurate with the hammer.

Chapter 7

Repairs to Brooches

Brooch repairs are mostly a matter of fitting new pins, joints (hinges), and catches. The commonest types of joints with their appropriate pins are shown.

The ball joint, Fig. 7-1, is the one commonly used on modern brooches and is obtainable ready-made in most precious metals. It is no great expense to keep a stock of silver and plated ones, but with gold it is often worthwhile to make your own. It is not possible to imitate the balled profile of the machine-made ones but a flat-sided one, though not so neat in appearance, works just as well.

Using a strip of the appropriate metal about 0.5mm thick and 3mm wide, bend it as shown in the Fig. 7-2 and press it tightly together. Drill the rivet hole before removing the surplus metal at the end because the joint can be gripped more firmly by the surplus piece. After the hole is drilled, remove the surplus by sawing where the dotted line is in Fig. 7-2. Grip the folded strip in the pliers and file down to the dotted line shown in Fig. 7-3. You will now have a joint with a matching piece for the pin. To allow free movement, the pieces should be rounded off as shown by the dotted lines in Fig. 7-4.

The joint in Fig. 7-5 is most common on older brooches. These are also obtainable ready-made and are cheap enough in base metal and silver, but when it comes to gold they can often be replaced with the homemade one just described. If not, it is a simple job to solder two pieces of tube into a small angle of sheet as shown in Fig. 7-6.

Fitting a new pin to this type of joint can often be a frustrating job, sometimes because a steel rivet was once fitted and has rusted in solid or the rivet was not tapered and has been kept in place by excessive hammering at both ends.

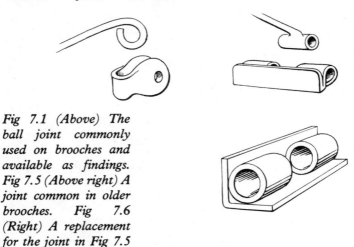

Fig 7.1 (Above) The ball joint commonly used on brooches and available as findings. Fig 7.5 (Above right) A joint common in older brooches. Fig 7.6 (Right) A replacement for the joint in Fig 7.5 can be made by soldering lengths of gold tube into a small piece of angled sheet, as below.

In the first case, a spot of penetrating oil or Three-in-One oil will help to loosen it. If the tubes are pinched with the flat pliers, this will stretch them a little and break the grip of the rust. In both cases, file away the ends of the rivet and decide whether or not it was tapered. If it was tapered, press against the small end with a blunt point. If you use something sharp like a scriber, it will dig in and tend to spread the end a little, thus defeating the object. With a

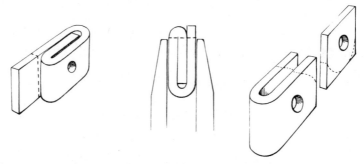

Fig 7.2 (Left) The first step in making a substitute for a gold joint. The surplus piece at the end is for gripping by pliers when drilling the hole. Fig 7.3 (Centre) After the hole is drilled, file off the end to the dotted line by holding the piece in pliers. Fig 7.4 (Right) The three pieces should now be shaped as shown by the dotted lines.

really awkward one, you may have to place it end-on over a piece of steel tube and tap the other end of the hinge pin with a punch. A graining tool with the end ground flat makes a good punch for this job. There are sets of matching tubes and punches used by watchmakers that are ideal for this and many other situations.

Select or make a pin with a matching tube. When this is fitted into the joint, insert a suitably sized broach and match and taper the inside of the tubes. Fit a brass or nickel taper pin, which should be a tight fit in the joint and a friction fit in the pin. You may have to broach the pin tube separately to achieve this result, but usually the greater area of contact of the joint is sufficient. Snip off the surplus and file the ends flat, leaving a little excess at the narrow end for riveting over. A professional-looking finish can be given to it if you leave a little excess at both ends and dome them with a large graining tool. If you do not have one large enough, soften an old one and file the end back until the diameter is right, then hollow it out with a dental burr. It is not necessary to reharden it as it will last a long time in its soft state.

Often a new pin will lack any spring tension because the soldering on of the tube has softened that end of the pin. This can be overcome by sliding a pin vice (Fig. 7-7) down the pin to within

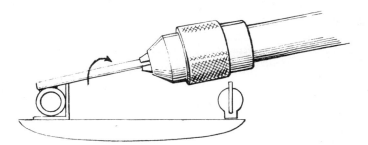

Fig 7.7 Hardening a new pin by twisting it in a pin vice.

about 5mm of the tube. Tighten it as firmly as possible, then carefully twist the pin. Usually half a turn is sufficient to harden the metal again.

The visor joint, shown in Fig. 7-8, does not crop up very often. Although ready-made pins are available, it is hardly worth keeping them in stock. You can usually make do with the pin in Fig. 7-9, which is formed from round wire using the round-nosed pliers.

The simple joint in Fig. 7-9 is usually found on cheap brooches only. On lead alloy paste brooches, it is part of the brooch and made of the same material, which makes it impossible to hammer over the end of the rivet, as the vibration enlarges the hole. The only solution is to run a little soft solder round one end of the rivet. If you remove the heat the instant the solder runs, you can usually avoid soldering the pin as well. If the solder does get to the pin, allow the brooch to cool. Then heat the pin a little way up from the joint, keeping a little tension on the pin so that it breaks free as soon as the solder is soft enough.

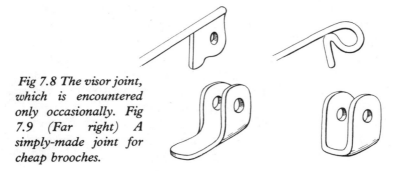

Fig 7.8 The visor joint, which is encountered only occasionally. Fig 7.9 (Far right) A simply-made joint for cheap brooches.

The four main types of brooch catch are illustrated in Fig. 7-10. There are many variations of these, but in principle they are the same. The first one, the simple hook catch, is the most common and often comes in for replacement. An ordinary jump ring bent to shape, and with a flat filed on it where it is soldered to the brooch, is the usual way to replace it. Make sure you curl the end in as shown in Fig. 7-10. This makes it more difficult for the pin to

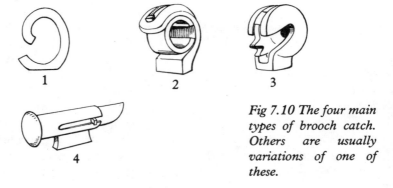

Fig 7.10 The four main types of brooch catch. Others are usually variations of one of these.

become accidentally unhooked and prevents it getting caught in the clothing.

The common fault with the other three - the safety catches - is that the moveable part works loose and becomes lost. The best cure is to fit a new catch, but if the soldering is going to endanger any stones or any other vulnerable part, it is better to cannibalise a new catch for a matching centrepiece. The parts are seldom a perfect match and you will have to fiddle around with them to get them working properly. That is why a complete replacement is better where possible.

Many older brooches, particularly hollow ones, will have been repaired with lead solder and the repair sometimes disguised by gilding or gold paint. With these, it will pay to scratch any suspicious looking patches of solder with a penknife. Usually the soldering has been done to avoid the removal and subsequent resetting of a stone or cameo which would not stand the heat of hard soldering and where such a course of action would turn a relatively simple and inexpensive repair into a much more costly one. Unfortunately, some customers, faced with an expensive repair, will accept the alternative of a comparatively cheap lead solder job to one costing ten times more. The customer does not know the difference and a trap is laid for the next repairer!

The commonest form of a lead solder repair on brooches is shown by the assisted joint and catch illustrated in Fig. 7-11. The joint or catch is hard-soldered to a large patch, which in turn is lead soldered to the brooch. The larger area of lead solder makes up for the weakness of the metal. These are easy enough to make, with the advantage that the patch can be tailored to match the outline of the brooch.

Even using such a safe method of replacing a joint and catch, there are pitfalls to watch for. The worst, in my opinion, is on the old silver Celtic style brooches, often made in the form of a circular shield inlaid with agate slices. They are invariably filled with pitch or shellac, which even the heat of melting lead solder will disturb. There is nothing more disheartening, having made a neat repair on the back of the brooch, than to turn it over and find all the stones neatly elevated from their holes on a small column of pitch. It is the devil's own job to get them back in their holes with all the surfaces level. So, as a general warning, beware of any stones that do not obviously appear to be held in by the metal of the setting. If the item seem to be made of solid metal and appears lighter than it should be, examine the edges of the stone with an eyeglass for the tell-tale line of adhesive. If it is there, it would be wiser to consider the use of epoxy resin in place of lead solder which, with the mating surfaces pecked rough with a graver, makes a very strong join.

One type of safety catch that can be made by hand is illustrated in Fig. 7-12. It is usually found on bar brooches, although it may be fitted on other types of small brooches. The restrictions of its use lie in the fact that it is necessary to get a finger well behind the brooch to open and close it. Consequently the larger the brooch the more difficult and fiddly it is.

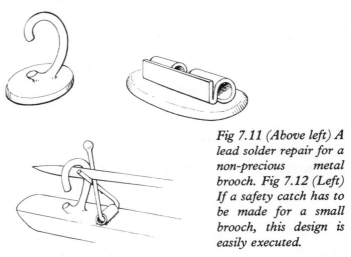

Fig 7.11 (Above left) A lead solder repair for a non-precious metal brooch. Fig 7.12 (Left) If a safety catch has to be made for a small brooch, this design is easily executed.

Solder a short length of tube to the brooch about 3mm from the catch. Pass a snug-fitting piece of wire through it and bend the wire into a cross as shown. The point where the two arms cross is adjusted so that the pin cannot escape from them once the catch is locked into position. The short arm is made as short as practical and the end smoothed. The large arm is left about 1mm over length. A dab of flux is applied to the end of it and another dab at the point of contact between the two arms. Heat the tip of the long arm to melting point so that a small bead is formed on the end, then run a piece of solder into the cross. If when trying out the catch, you find it is too tight or too loose, raise or lower the top of the catch slightly until it operates like a light switch, with a neat click. If it is not practical to bend the catch you can either put a slight kink in the safety catch to lower it, or bow the pin a little to obtain the desired effect.

Problems with Lockets

The main problems with lockets, apart from the suspension loop becoming worn, are with the hinge and catch. Most of them are held closed by the inner bezel being a tight fit inside the front. With use, the edge of this bezel wears, away allowing the front to flop open. The fault is remedied by burnishing the inside edge until it is reshaped and holds the front again. It is usually only necessary to burnish the portion opposite the hinge to make it secure as shown in Fig. 7-13.

To replace a worn or broken hinge of the type shown in Fig. 7-14, it is first necessary to remove the taper pin and then the old tubes. As with watchcase hinges (page 120), if the pin refuses to budge, burnish the exposed parts of the tubes. A suitable burnisher can be made from a graining tool if the tapered part and half of the stem is smoothed with emery, then polishing paper, and given a final polish on the polishing machine. All scratches should be removed because they will act like a cutting edge and remove metal instead of stretching it.

With the pin removed, it is sometimes possible to flux and heat the tubes and pluck or flick them off when the solder has melted. Failing that, they will have to be sawn off to leave about half the tube. The rest can be filed away with a rat-tail file, being careful not to widen the channel in which the tube rests.

Replace the outside tubes first. If the channel in which they fit is not very long or deep, it will be difficult to solder the two tubes in perfect alignment. In this case, use one piece of tube the whole

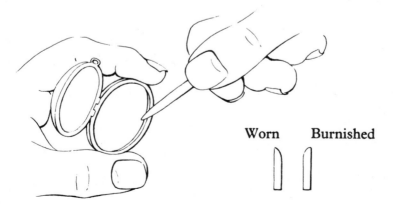

Worn   Burnished

Fig 7.13 Making a locket catch work by burnishing to reshape the edge.

length of the hinge and cut away the centre portion after if has been soldered in position. After cutting a new centre piece of tube and making it a perfect fit between the outer two, solder it in position, pickle and clean the two halves of the locket and fit them together. The tubes should be in perfect alignment when the locket is closed. If they are, a taper can be broached in them and a taper pin fitted. The ends of the hinge should then be filed and smoothed to match the contours of the locket. If the tubes are not in alignment when the locket is closed, it is no use opening it to get them in line while you fit the pin. Even if you manage to close it afterwards, the halves will be under tension and spring open at a touch. The centre tube will have to be heated and moved until it lines up with the outer two when closed.

The taper pin should be a good tight fit in the outer two tubes and a friction fit in the centre one. On oval and round lockets, the ends of the hinge will have to filed at an angle to match the curve of the locket. If the pin is not a tight fit in the outer tubes, it may turn and expose a sharp point at each end of the hinge as shown in Fig. 7-15. To avoid this happening, some lockets and watchcases are fitted with a short taper pin and the ends of the hinge are fitted with a plug of metal to match the case shown in section in Fig. 7-16. Look out for this when removing hinge pins. If you suspect that plugs have been so fitted, dig into the sloping end with a graver and you will find that you can lever them out.

The high points on old embossed lockets have sometimes become worn right through and the holes filled with lead solder, so examine any of this type carefully before carrying out any hard soldering. Another old type of locket has the back and front made of gold, but the rims carrying the hinge and catch were made of

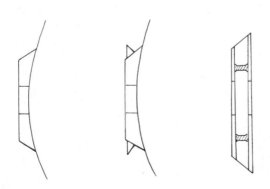

Fig 7.14 (Left) A locket hinge. Fig 7.15 (Centre) A hinge pin that turns will catch on clothing. Fig 7.16 An arrangement that prevents the situation in Fig 7.15. The pin is short and the ends are plugged.

base metal and the backs and rims were sometimes lead soldered together.

Earrings

The five main types of pierced ear fitting and the two for non-pierced ears are shown in Fig. 7-17. All of them are quite simple and any repairs are usually obvious. Replacement clips for the French fittings (Fig. 7-17 No.1) are always bought ready-made, although occasionally an 18ct one is required, in which case it is worth making one from a piece of strip rather than buy in quantity.

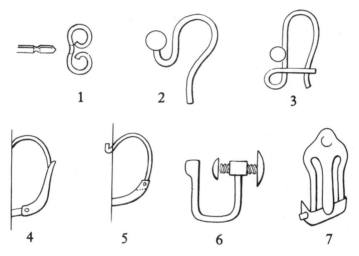

Fig 7.17 The five main types of fittings for pierced ears. The last two, lower right, are for non-pierced ears.

The strip should be 20mm long (7.8 in) and 3.5mm wide. It should be left springy from the rollers, but not so hard that it is liable to crack when bent. The hole is pierced by hammering a point through the strip while supported on a piece of hard wood as shown in Fig. 7-18. This way the hole is indented as shown, and forms a guide for the peg. The scrolls are bent up with the round-nosed pliers until they touch. Then the hole is enlarged with a broach which at the same time forms a slight groove in the scrolls so that they will stay square on the peg (Fig. 7-19).

When a clip has been lost, it is usually because there is no safety groove on the peg. In this case, hold the last 2mm of the peg in a pin vice (Fig. 7-20) and file a groove round it with a rat-tail file, using the jaws of the pin vice as a guide. If the clip works its way along the peg, the scrolls will drop into this groove and stay put. Without it, they work their way over the end and are lost.

The spring-loaded guard (Fig. 7-17 No.4) loses its tension with wear. It can be given a new lease on life by increasing the curve with the round-nosed pliers so that the leaf spring is in firm contact with the base again.

The type of fitting shown in Fig. 7-17 No. 5 is usually only found on antique earrings. Its two main faults are: the hinge breaks or the hole where the hook fits becomes so enlarged that the hook will not catch. The usual remedy for the second fault is to solder a small ring over the hole to reduce its diameter. When the hinge breaks it is usually the centre leaf that fails at the base or across the hole. If it is broken at the base, it can be soldered without disturbing the hinge if fully opened as shown in Fig. 7-21. If it is broken across the hole, it it best to fit a new centre leaf. Cut a slot in the base of the hook to take the new centre leaf rather than butt soldering it on.

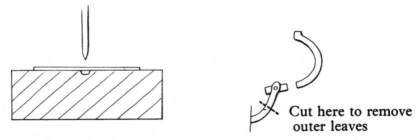

Cut here to remove
outer leaves

Fig 7.18 (Left) Piercing a hole with a punch on a piece of indented hard wood will provide a guide for the peg. Fig 7.21 A form of clip found on some antique earrings. If broken at the bottom it can be resoldered. If the outer leaves are broken, they should be cut where indicated by the dotted line.

If the outer leaves of the hinge are broken, cut them both off as shown in Fig. 7-21, well clear of the bottom of the hinge. A matching piece of wire can then be held in the pin vice while a slot is cut in it for the hinges. The bottom of the slot should be at an angle to match the angle on the centre leaf (see dotted line in Fig. 7-17, No 5). It is as well to drill the pin hole before cutting the slot. If you remove the whole of the wire right down to the earring, you would have to heat the earring in order to solder on the new piece. Often these earrings are set with heat-sensitive stones, are hollow, or

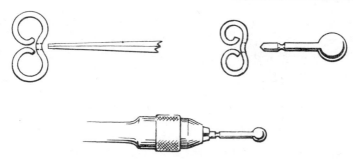

Fig 7.19 (Top) The hole should be enlarged with a broach. The broach should also cut shallow grooves in the scrolls to hold the peg centrally. Fig 7.20 As a safety device, a groove should also be formed around the pin where the scrolls grip it. Use a pin vice and rat tail file.

have a fine gold matt finish which can easily be damaged. Much Victorian jewellery has such a finish, achieved by repeatedly heating and quenching the article in acid so that the base metal is dissolved out of the alloy, leaving a layer of fine gold on the surface. (It was called 'depletion gilding' and was used as early as the 15th century by South American Indians). Once damaged, this surface is impossible to restore effectively.

The threads on the earscrews in (Fig. 7-17 No. 6) become worn so they cannot be tightened properly. If the base of the tube is pinched with the flat-nosed pliers, this will reduce the diameter of the tube and tighten the screw.

Clips in Fig. 7-17 No. 7 can be tightened either by bending them a little so that the centre spring leaf comes into contact with the base again, or by removing the clip and re-tensioning by tapping the base of the centre leaf with a hammer to work-harden it and make it springy again, then refitting it.

One job that crops up fairly frequently is refitting pearls on to stud earrings. The most common cause of pearls coming off is because the area where the adhesive is placed was left smooth or polished. Before applying a new layer of epoxy resin, file a small cross over the hole in the pearl as shown in Fig. 7-22. Also, roughen the inside of the cup with a graver or dental burr and lightly crimp the peg that goes into the hole in the pearl. This provides a key for the adhesive and increases the area of contact.

Some drop earrings are merely one or more gemstone beads or pearls threaded on to a piece of wire. When the loop at the top wears out, the stones prevent a new loop being soldered on, so a new wire has to be made. A suitable length of wire should be fluxed and heated at one end until a small bead is formed. The wire is then pickled and cleaned and pushed into the tightest hole in the draw-plate from the front. The bead is then hammered into a flat pinhead which will support the beads without being visible from the front as in Fig. 7-23. The beads are threaded back on to the wire and a loop formed on the other end with the round-nosed pliers.

Hinged sleeper earrings sometimes come in for repair when the hinge is broken. It is only practical to repair them if the centre leaf has broken off at the base. They can then be repaired in the same way as already described for No 5 in Fig. 7-17. The wire they are made from is usually too thin for the outside leaves to be repaired.

If any hollow dome studs come in for repair, usually to have the peg soldered back on, check that they have a ventilation hole before heating them and make one if necessary. They do not always explode when heated, but there is no way of finding out which will and which will not. When the halves were soldered together originally the air inside expanded and the excess was forced out. When the solder has sealed the joint, the earrings cool and the air inside cools to form a partial vacuum. If the vacuum remains intact, the earring will not explode when reheated, but a hole too small to be seen with a lens will allow the air to seep back again over a period of time. However, such a hole will be too small to cope with the rapid expansion of the air when the earring is reheated and it will explode. Apart from frightening the life out of the repairer, it can be very dangerous. It is like having a firecracker go off six inches from your nose; I did a backward somersault through a hardboard partition when it first happened to me, so always make sure there is a ventilation hole.

Removing Dents

Sometimes these earrings will arrive squashed or dented. If you can pull them apart successfully, they can be reshaped in a doming block using a doming punch. A block and punch are shown in Fig. 7-24. There is a punch to suit each size of dome. A makeshift block for small domes can be made by cutting a series of hollows in a piece of brass with different sized ball-shaped dental burrs and using rounded off nails for punches. The only limit is the size of your largest burr.

If only one of a pair of hollow dome stud earrings is damaged and cannot be repaired, a new one can be made from two discs of identical diameter. When one has been domed to match the existing earring, its diameter will be much less than that of the remaining disc, so there will be a rim when they are placed together. The rim can be held by tweezers and *paillons* of solder placed on it as shown in Fig. 7-25, making the soldering job quite simple.

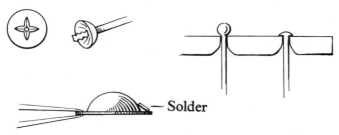

Fig 7.22 (Top left) A small cross filed over the blind hole in a pearl to key the adhesive when the peg on the left is inserted. Fig 7.23 Forming a head on the end of wire to hold beads on drop earrings. A bead formed by melting is flattened by using a draw plate and small hammer. Fig 7.25 How to solder a dome onto a backing plate.

The disc that has to be domed should be softened by annealing and given a shallow dome first, moving in three steps to the final shape. It may be necessary to resoften the metal before the final shape can be achieved. After the halves are soldered together, snip off the rim, but do not file the edge smooth until the peg has been soldered in position. If you file and emery it before fitting the peg, when the solder is reheated it will be drawn into the dome slightly and the join will become visible, making it necessary to file and emery it once more.

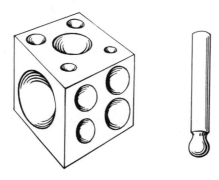

Fig 7.24 Domed earrings can be repaired or replaced by the use of a doming block and punch.

Pendants

Virtually anything can be hung from a chain and called a pendant, there are no repairs that apply specifically to pendants. The most common repair is the replacement of worn loops and suspension rings, which is quite straightforward. The precautions to protect heat sensitive stones and delicate finishes apply to pendants as to any other piece of jewellery.

You might sometime be given a coin to mount as a pendant. Usually no soldering can be done on the actual coin, in which case it can either be treated like a gemstone and mounted in claws soldered to a backing wire, or fitted into a circular channel. How to make a claw mount should be obvious by now, but the channel will need some explanation.

A disc of metal brass or something harder, the same diameter and thickness as the coin will be needed. Then cut a strip of the metal chosen for the mount so that it is three times the thickness of the coin in width, 0.012 in thick, and with a length equal to the circumference of the coin. This is bent into a circle and butt soldered. The coin should be a tight fit into it.

Press the disc of metal midway into the circle and place it over another piece of metal of the same thickness as the disc. This is to act as a support for the disc and keep it in its midway position. Next you need a washer that is a tight fit over the outside of the circle of metal. This is pushed midway down the outside to coincide with the disc on the inside. The set-up should be as shown in section in Fig. 7-26. The metal strip should be in an annealed state. The assembly is placed on a steel bench block and the top edge of the strip hammered down over the disc. Tap it down a little at a time, working your way round it gradually to avoid kinking the strip (Fig. 7-27). When the rim is hammered flat on the disc as shown, turn it over and do the same to the other edge. The supporting piece under the disc will not be necessary this time. If you find that the edges have become springy and will not be hammered flat down on the disc, heat them a little with the propane torch, but not so much as to melt the solder, and try again.

When the mount is flat both sides, emery out any hammer marks and remove the washer. Saw through the soldered join and remove the disc. Check that the coin is a good fit in the mount. The mount may be a little oversize, in which case cut a small section from one end until it grips the coin when the ends meet.

The mount should be finished off cheaply by fitting two loops as

Fig 7.26 Stages in making a grooved holder for a coin used as a pendant, seen in section. A shallow cylinder of metal is first given a top rim, using a thinner support underneath it. The completed holder is seen in Fig 7.28.

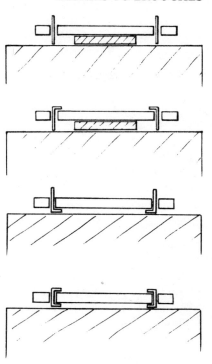

shown in Fig. 7-28 and on the right in Fig. 7- 29, which overlap when the mount is closed and are locked together by inserting a large jump ring through them. Alternatively, a more decorative mount may be applied, as shown on the left in Fig. 7-29, with the

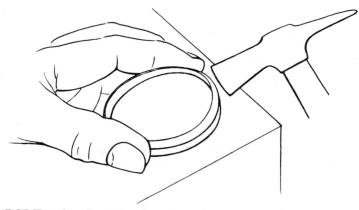

Fig 7.27 Tapping down the rim a little at a time to avoid kinking. Note outer ring omitted for clarity.

Fig 7.28 The normal way of providing a fastener for a coin holder, shown open and closed. The loops are held together by a large jump ring passing through them. Fig 7.29 (Right) A decorative mount for the coin holder.

two loops on top of the scrolls and a jump ring fitted as before. The scrolls are best made from square or round wire, rolled into a strip rather than cut from sheet. The second method always leaves a distorted edge which is difficult to remove.

If you are in a hurry, the washer can be dispensed with, but you will end up with a rounded outer edge on to which it is difficult to solder the scrolls.

Cuff Links

The three common types of cuff link fittings are shown in Fig. 7-30. The chain type often require new end loops and chains, which is a straightforward job. The chains are usually five links long and can be made from oval jump rings. Remember that wear on the links has made the chain a good deal longer than necessary, so do

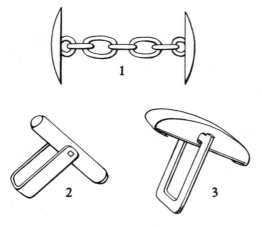

Fig 7.30 A chain cuff link (top), which will lengthen with wear, and two click over types, without their heads.

not aim to make the new chain the same length. Watch out for hollow torpedo or dumbell ends. Make certain each has a ventilation hole before heating it.

The click-over cuff links (No. 2 and No. 3 in Fig. 7-30) sometimes break away from the head and you will have to remove the moveable part before soldering to avoid softening the spring. On the tubular ones, No 2, the square centre pin is riveted over slightly and one end will have to be filed down before the pin can be pulled through and the tube removed. With the other type, No.3, it is just a matter of bending back the end flaps to remove the swivel bar. In both cases, gold cuff-links can often be kept cool enough for soldering if wrapped in wet cotton wool, but silver ones will have to be taken apart.

Stick Pins

The only thing peculiar to stick pins is the pin itself. If a pin is broken, it should be rejoined with a lap join. If a replacement pin is required, and there is a twist in it, flatten the middle by hammering on a piece of bar. Alternatively, thread the pin half way through the flat rollers, clamp them and roll just the centre ½ in or so to about half the thickness of the pin. After annealing, the pin can be held in two pairs of flat pliers in order to twist it. The twisted part will be thicker than the plain part, and should be filed down until it matches. The twist helps to prevent the pin working its way loose.

Chapter 8

Some Unusual Jobs and How to Tackle Them

Job No 1. Description: Two hallmarked 22ct wedding rings. Instructions: Two wedding rings to be made into one, same width and size as broadest one but thicker.

The first thing to do is to make a note of the size required then weigh the two rings. Write this information on the job packet in case there are any complaints later. A heavier ring tends to feel loose on the finger so you might be accused of making it the wrong size. Also two rings always look as if they contain more metal than the single finished ring.

If the customer is expecting the finished ring to be the same weight as the original two, some gold will have to be added to allow for filing and waste ends. In this case 2 grams should suffice. This is noted on the packet and taken into account when pricing.

The 3/16 in square ingot mould will just accommodate the width of the new ring and it is clamped together to produce an ingot ⅛ by 3/16 in. Gold of 22ct and 18ct as well, being much denser than 9ct, will flow easily into narrow cavities where 9ct and silver would not. The gold plus the extra 2 grams is melted and poured into the mould and the resulting ingot pickled and dried.

No half-round roller the exact size is available, so the ingot is put through one slightly oversize and brought to as near the finished profile as possible so that the minimum amount of filing is necessary, resulting in the minimum amount of waste. This is most important when working with the more expensive metals. Although the filings are collected and eventually turned into cash at the bullion dealers, there is a significant difference between the price he pays you for it and what he charges you for new metal.

Even so, over a year, the amount collected, though it does not amount to a great deal, can add up to a week's wage. So remember that every time you wield the file you are converting usable metal into unusable metal.

Ring Bending

Though it is not difficult to bend the 22ct strip into a ring using the ring pliers, you can get a much more perfect circle using the ring bending machine illustrated in Fig. 8-1. It really comes into its

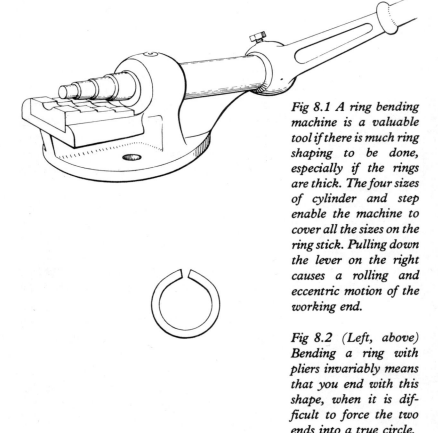

Fig 8.1 A ring bending machine is a valuable tool if there is much ring shaping to be done, especially if the rings are thick. The four sizes of cylinder and step enable the machine to cover all the sizes on the ring stick. Pulling down the lever on the right causes a rolling and eccentric motion of the working end.

Fig 8.2 (Left, above) Bending a ring with pliers invariably means that you end with this shape, when it is difficult to force the two ends into a true circle.

own if you have a heavy 9ct ring to bend. With pliers, you invariably end up with the shape shown in Fig. 8-2 because you have nothing to lever against when you get to the end, making it a struggle to get the ends to meet while still having a reasonably circular ring. The extra leverage the machine provides overcomes this with ease.

The block in Fig. 8-1 has four steps cut at different radii which enable you to cover the range of sizes on the stick. The in-between sizes are obtained by not pressing the lever fully down when forming the ring.

Before bending, the strip of gold is cut down to 2 7/16in (62 mm) which will give size 'P' with a fraction over for squaring the ends. The end of the strip is laid in the centre step and the lever lowered and pressed lightly, just sufficient to bend the strip without marking it. Then the lever is lifted, the strip moved forward a short distance, and the lever pressed again. The shorter the distance the strip is moved forward, the smoother the curve of the ring.

If the ends of the ring do not meet when the strip has passed through the machine, it can be given one or two presses in the smaller step or finished off with the ring pliers.

With the ends squared up and closed, the join is fluxed and a large piece of 22ct solder put in place. I said a large piece because the solder used for 22ct gold is actually .800 (19.2ct) and is not as flexible as 22ct, so if there is any stretching to do, the ring will break at the join unless there is some excess solder to strengthen it.

With the ring soldered and pickled, the excess solder is filed away from the inside only; then the ring shaped up on the triblet. If the size is correct, the join is cleaned up and all marks and scratches filed out. It is finished with the emery stick and finally polished. If the ring is oversize, the excess solder on the outside of the ring will have to be removed before the ring is compressed in the sizing machine. It only requires a little pressure on either the Pinfold or vertical sizing machine to make a large reduction in the size. Be very careful, otherwise you may have to stretch the ring again and without the excess solder on the outside there is the possibility of it breaking at the join necessitating resoldering. Apart from the fact that 22ct solder is expensive, the join seldom breaks cleanly. The ends tend to contract and stretch thinner than the rest of the ring before breaking in a jagged end. This means that a considerable amount of metal has to be removed in order to make the ends match again, which in turn means more stretching or a piece added to the ring. You end up with a messy job, all because of insufficient care when reducing the ring.

Job No 2. Description: Gents gold stone-set signet. Oval bloodstone loose in the packet.
Instructions: Reset stone.

The ring has had a lot of wear: ring and stone are badly scratched. After placing the stone back in the setting you can see why it has come out. What little metal was holding it in originally has worn away. There is usually a choice of raising the setting or lowering the stone, but in this case there is no setting as such. The stone was let flush into the ring and the edge of the hole hammered over the stone, leaving a perfectly smooth surface right up to the stone. It is not feasible to flush solder round the edge of the hole because even if you could get the solder to run where you wanted it to, it is more brittle than the parent metal and would not stand hammering over the stone.

The back support for the stone is lowered all round by cutting it away with a round burr in the pendant drill until there is sufficient metal above the sloping edge of the stone to hammer on to it - 0.5 mm is sufficient.

Ideally the next part requires three hands: One to grip the ring clamps holding the ring, one to guide a small flat-ended punch round the edge of the setting, and another to hit it with the hammer.

Without the extra hand, the clamps will have to be held in the bench vice as in Fig. 8-3. The hammer blows should be light and even and the indentations made by the punch should overlap so that the end result is a slight recess all round the stone which causes the edge to spread over and on to it. When the stone is secure and does not rattle when tapped with the finger, the surrounding metal is filed down until the recess vanishes and only the small lip retaining the stone remains.

Job No 3. Description: Single stone 18ct yellow gold shank and platinum claw setting. It would have originally held a half carat stone. Included in the packet is a 0.05ct diamond.
Instructions: Fit small stone using illusion setting.

First a disc of 18ct white gold or platinum is made and set in the ring in the same way as the original stone and the tip of each claw soldered in place. A guide hole is drilled in the centre and widened with a round burr so that the stone is a tight fit with enough metal

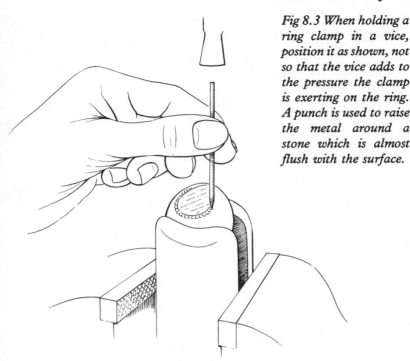

Fig 8.3 When holding a ring clamp in a vice, position it as shown, not so that the vice adds to the pressure the clamp is exerting on the ring. A punch is used to raise the metal around a stone which is almost flush with the surface.

above the girdle of the stone to allow for setting. With the stone in position, six grains are dug out of the edge of the metal surrounding the stone at a position midway between two of the original claws as shown in Fig. 8-4. As with the star setting (page 106), work your way round them levering them over a little at a time until the stone is secure. Then round off the grains with a graining tool.

Using the chisel graver, well sharpened and polished, place one corner just clear of the stone and midway between two grains. Aim

Fig 8.4 (Left) An illusion setting - the stone is set in the middle of a platinum or white gold disc, which is itself facetted and mounted in claws to increase the apparent area of the stone. The first cuts to be made are shown shaded.

the graver so that it just misses the claw and hold it tilted at such an angle that the other edge of the cut finishes midway between two outer claws as shown in Fig. 8-5. Tilting the graver in the opposite direction and starting from the same point, aim for the other side of the claw. When this has been done to all the claws, a six-pointed star will have been formed with the stone at the centre as in Fig. 8-4.

Fig 8.5 (Right) Making the first cuts with a chisel graver, after marking the centre points between the original claws and join-ing them to the centre points between the stone claws, as shown by the dotted line.

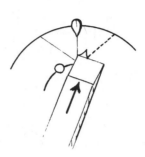

Scribe a guide line from each inner grain to the point of the star, dividing each arm down the middle. The next bit is the trickiest. With the graver tilted, begin the cut at the point shown and cut down to the scribed line. Then repeat from the other side of the grain. Begin the cut with the graver pointing towards the point of the star until you are clear of the grain and in no danger of chopping it off. Then move it round until the cutting edge is parallel to the scribed line. Cut downwards at a shallow angle up to the line as in Fig. 8-6. When the same is done from the other side, the piece of metal should click out leaving the arm of the star indented.

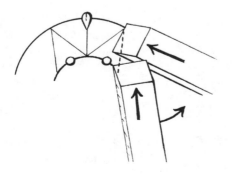

Fig 8.6 (Left) Cutting the facets of the inner star is more difficult because of the necessity of avoiding the smaller claws holding the stone by twisting the graver.

You can get the angle even and more accurate by starting at the point of the star and cutting towards the grain, but if you slip you are in danger of cutting off the grain.

When all the cuts are completed, the setting should be as shown in Fig. 8-7. A very light polishing with the bristle brush is all that is necessary to complete it.

The graver should be kept sharp and well polished so that the minimum of pressure is needed and you can concentrate on guiding the graver without having to control the pressure on it. If you find yourself having to push too hard, try grinding the point of the graver to a more acute angle.

Fig 8.7 (Right) The second cuts are shown shaded. When all cuts are completed, the illusion setting should look like this.

Job No 4. Description: 9ct yellow gold Star of David, pierced and with a wriggled pattern. Top V-piece and loop missing.
Instructions: Replace missing part of star pendant.

This job is included because, although it is simple enough to make a small V and solder it in place, matching up the pattern is not, unless you know how to do it.

Wriggling, as it is called, is often used as a decoration on lockets, pendants, hollow and solid bangles and it is often necessary to match up the pattern after you have worked on the article. It is done with the chisel-ended graver and to do it well and without slipping, the graver should have a keen edge. The edge should be straight and at right angles to the body of the graver. Hurried sharpening often leaves it bowed or sloping and in either case will defeat your best efforts at wriggling.

The action used I can only describe as similar to moving a wardrobe: you tilt it on one narrow side and 'walk' it across the room.

If you dig the graver in and walk it forward it will dig out a series of opposing triangles as shown in Fig. 8-8. Do not press downwards, the weight of the hand should make a deep enough cut. The big mistake beginners make is not to tilt the graver an equal amount in each direction. There is a tendency with right-handed people to tilt more in the outward direction than the inward, making it difficult to follow a line so that the pattern becomes uneven. If you do it slowly to begin with and watch your hand to see that it tilts an equal amount in each direction, you will quickly get the hang of it.

Fig 8.8 A wriggle cut is a simple way of engraving broad lines. A chisel graver, right, is used and 'walked' to make it cut zig-zags, by rocking it from corner to corner while gently pushing forward. The movement of the graver is shown on the letter E, right. If shading is needed, this is done by cutting a bevel at the edge of the wriggled line so that the incline is down from the wriggled line as far right, not the other way.

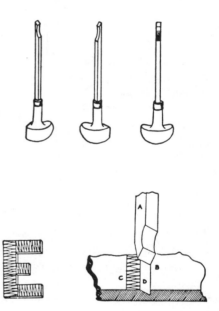

Engraving Letters

It is possible to engrave letters using this method, without the hours of practice an engraver needs, in order to control the tool, because you just 'walk' it round the curves and corners (See Engraving on Precious Metals, N.A.G. Press).

To make intricate designs and engrave lettering, you must be able to grip the item firmly and rotate it in any direction. The cheap and easy solution to this is to lop another 4 in off your broom handle - if you have any left - file one end flat and coat it with shellac or sealing wax. The item to be engraved is warmed and set into the shellac and will be gripped firmly enough to withstand the pressures of engraving. The broom handle provides the engraver with a good grip on the work.

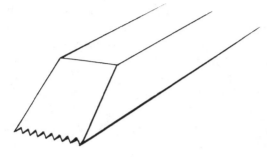

Fig 8.9 A graving tool known as a 'liner' for hatching and cross hatching. It has a corrugated cutting edge. Solder is strongly attracted to cross hatched lines and a liner may be needed to restore them.

There is an engraving tool called a liner, which is a chisel graver with the underside corrugated as shown in Fig. 8-9. You can wriggle with this and get a different effect but its greatest use lies in cross-hatching and background work. Solder runs down engraved lines with great enthusiasm and this may happen during repair. Single lines can be cleaned with the square graver but to renew cross-hatching and some matt backgrounds on medals and signets, the liner is a great help. By digging out small (2 mm) lengths with the liner in random directions, a very interesting background can be produced.

Job No 5. Description: Antique three-stone claw-set yellow gold ring containing three oval turquoise. Two stones very dark.
Instructions: Replace dark stones for matching ones.

Turquoise is absorbent to a degree and with age and use, or misuse, grease tends to discolour it, turning it to a dark green. Sometimes, if the discoloration is not too great, a session in the ultrasonic cleaner with a fresh batch of cleaning fluid will clean and lighten it sufficiently. In the case of this ring the treatment was not very effective so the stones were removed from their settings, measured and replacements sent for. When they arrived, they would not seat properly in the settings because the backs were perfectly flat, whereas the originals had a fairly deep bevel round the edge. To cut a bevel with the emery stick or diamond wheel would have reduced their diameter too much so that they would have dropped through the settings.

I tried running the emery stick over the originals to find out how deep the discoloration was and discovered that it could be removed without lowering the dome of the stone too much. I shellaced the stones on to the heads of two ordinary flat-topped nails so that they could be rotated while they were being 'emeried', to keep a smooth curve on the stones free of flats. When the discoloration had been removed, the stones were repolished with a piece of polishing paper held in the palm of the hand. This treatment will usually only work with turquoise or softer gem materials such as coral and amber. Coral cabochons darken with age for the same reasons as turquoise. Softer stones that are not absorbent often become badly scratched. The scratches can also be removed in this manner.

Repolishing Stones
Harder stones require a different treatment. Opals are the most common stones that require repolishing but cabochon garnets, agates and tiger's-eye set in gents rings often get rough treatment and require repolishing.

Though it is not an expensive job if you can find the right firm to do it, it is immensely satisfying to be able to do it yourself, particularly if you get an opal whose surface has worn to a matt finish so that the colour is hardly visible and you can watch the brilliant colours come to life again as you polish it.

The basic requirements are a vertical, motor-driven spindle rotating at approximately 700 rpm, two 6 in (15 cm) diameter plywood discs covered with a thin layer of plastic foam and a 6 inch (15 cm) diameter felt buff.

The ready-made item is available among lapidary equipment. It comprises a cast aluminium pan containing a vertical spindle running in sealed ball bearings and having a water supply, drain cock and a stepped pulley beneath for varying the speed. However, for the small amount of use it is likely to get, the expense can hardly be justified.

If you have a power drill with a slow speed you can make do with that by mounting it on the bench and making arbors from nuts and bolts for the plywood discs and buff so they can be held in the chuck. The speed may be slightly higher than the ideal 700 rpm but this can be compensated for by using smaller diameter discs and buff or just using the inner part of the discs where the cutting rate will be lower and the stone will not become overheated.

Wet and dry emery discs of 320 grit and 400 grit are glued to the foam on the plywood discs. They can be bought ready made or cut from the squares sold for car body work.

You will need some water in a 'squeezy' bottle and some form of guard around the disc to prevent the water being thrown all over you and the workshop.

If the stone is out of the setting, it will have to be shellaced on to the end of a short length of dowel so it can be easily manipulated while in contact with the emery disc, otherwise you will end up with a series of flats instead of a smooth dome. If it is still in the setting, it can usually be polished in situ because the worst scratches are on the top of the dome, whereas near the setting the polish is intact so that you will not need to polish down the sides and risk wearing the settings away.

With the large stones made from a variety of quartz, such as agate and tiger's-eye, you will need to start off on the 320 grit disc and apply a certain amount of pressure to get rid of the deep scratches, but with opal and similar 'soft' stones which are usually small (10 mm by 8 mm downwards) it is best to try them on the 400 grit disc first to avoid removing too much of the stone. If this is not coarse enough to remove the scratches, use a worn 320 grit disc. A new one will cut away opal at a fairly rapid rate.

With the disc rotating and dampened with water, bring the stone into contact with it and constantly move it about, at the same time keeping a steady drip of water falling just in front of the stone so that there is no chance of it becoming overheated. Apart from heat damaging the stone, it can soften the shellac so that the stone flies off. When all the scratches are gone and you have a uniform matt finish, change over to the 400 grit disc and repeat the process. If you started with the 400 grit disc, finish on the most worn part of the disc. When changing from one disc to another, always rinse off any sludge or grit adhering to the stone or shellac.

Sometimes quite a good polish can be achieved on a well worn 400 grit disc, but it does not compare to the brilliance you can achieve on the felt buff using cerium oxide. This is a pink powder that can be purchased from mineral or hobby shops. It is quite cheap considering how long it lasts. It is mixed with water into a slurry and rubbed on to the surface of the buff with a clean finger while the buff is stationary. If you do not rub it in slightly, it will fly off when the buff rotates.

Opals will only need to be in contact with the buff for a very short while to achieve a good polish. Stones heat up very rapidly on the buff so only keep them in contact for a few seconds at a time. Make sure there is no grit or dirt on the stone or your fingers before using the buff. When it is not in use, keep the buff in a plastic bag to prevent any contamination.

Job No 6. Description: Silver handled button hook. The hook is very loose in the handle.
Instructions: Re-secure hook in handle.

As with many items of this type, the working part has a tang like a file and the handle is full of hard black wax. It is put together by heating the tang and forcing it into the wax. In this case a lot of the wax was missing so I packed the hole in the wax with flake shellac then heated the tang to just above the melting point of the shellac then pressed it in. Hold it in position for a short while to allow the shellac to melt and combine with the wax then harden. Do not overheat the tang or it will cause the wax to overheat and expand and force its way out of the handle. When the remainder has cooled and contracted, there will not be enough left to secure the tang properly.

Many silver-handled cutlery, paper knives etc. are put together in this way. Watch out for holes worn through the silver at the high points. If the wax becomes overheated it will shoot out of these and a blob of hot wax on the hand will make your eyes water and gain you the reputation of being foul-mouthed.

Job No 7. Description: Single stone, illusion set, 0.10ct diamond ring.
Instructions: Reset diamond.

The setting appears to be in good condition with no grains missing, so why and how did the stone come out? When it is put back on the setting the stone sits on the four grains and will not go into the hole. I lifted the grains a little and tried again. This time it went past the grains through the hole and down into the cage of the setting. There is no back support for the stone. The stone must have worked loose sometime in the past and have been rotating in the setting until it wore away the seating. It dropped into the cage, turned sideways and came out again between the grains. The original seating must have been very inadequate for that to happen, or else the bottom edge of the girdle had a much better cutting edge on it than the top.

To cure it I drilled the hole of the setting slightly larger and fitted and soldered a short length of 18ct white gold tube into it. This was filed down level with the setting and a seating for the stone cut into it with a round burr the same diameter as the stone. After pickling, the stone was fitted into the hole and six instead of four new grains dug out of the edge of the tube and pushed over the stone then rounded off with a graining tool. The remaining edges of the tube were matched to the illusion setting with a polished chisel graver.

Job No 8. Description: Two stone cross-over ring, white metal. Instructions: Size to ½.

This appeared to be a straightforward job at first glance: two ten-point diamonds in an all-white gold ring. I looked for the hallmark but all I could find was '333' stamped on the inside of the shank which did not convey anything to me but aroused some doubts. I weighed the ring in my hand and decided it could not be 18ct or platinum; it was too light. The metal was too blue-white for 9ct white gold or silver, but it could be rhodium-plated on either of these metals, in which case the stones were most unlikely to be diamonds. I examined the stones with an eyeglass. They were pure white and flawless, perfectly cut and identical; much too good had they been diamonds to be mounted in 9ct or silver, so I assumed them to be cubic zirconia, otherwise known as CZ. These will stand sizing heat, even in silver, but if they get overheated they turn permanently yellow. The stones would stand the heat but their rhodium-plated settings would become dark grey and extremely difficult to clean, so the head was wrapped in wet cotton wool.

When the shank was heated, it turned a blueish colour before eventually becoming dark grey, which indicated that it was rhodium-plated. The plating on the shank would be removed with the emerying and polishing but that did not matter as the metal beneath was white. Judging by the speed the heat reached the cotton wool, the metal must have been silver, so I used silver solder on

165

the join and was fortunate enough to get it to run before the cotton wool dried out and the settings became discoloured. When the ring was eventually polished, the difference in colour between the plated settings and the silver shank was hardly noticeable.

Job No 9. Description: Six-stone diamond and 18ct white gold ring of modern design.
Instructions: Repair all settings.

The ring was not hallmarked but stamped 18ct and judging by the weight the stamp was telling the truth. To confirm this, the stones were examined and judged to be diamonds. None showed any signs of wear; they were unevenly cut and varied slightly in colour. The largest, a 0.15ct centre stone, had visible flaws in it.

The head of the ring consisted of a series of irregular shaped 'logs' diminishing in length towards the shoulders. The six settings were four-clawed and placed randomly over the 'logs'. I looked closely at the base of the settings to see if they were a part of the head or had been soldered on separately and discovered they were part of the head. Had they been separate, the solder would have melted had I tried to rebuild the claws and the settings would perhaps have moved or fallen off. Next I looked at the sides and the back of the head. Judging by the angle at which the sides sloped inwards towards the finger, it would be a difficult ring to make in one piece but relatively easy in two. I found a line of lighter-coloured solder attaching the head to the sides and the shank, so I would have to be careful not to put any pressure on the head when it was heated in case the solder became soft enough for the head to move.

The tips on the large centre stone were nearly gone, so that could be removed from its setting for safety and the claws rebuilt. The small ones were so placed that it would be impossible to use a file in the right place in order to shape up any new tips, so I decided to remove the stones one at a time, stretch the claws and reset the stones, then thicken all the stretched tips with solder to reduce filing to an absolute minimum.

This job, like the last one, is an example of how a thorough examination and thinking ahead pays off. After you have sat a few times with tears rolling down your cheeks and a misshapen chunk of metal in the tweezers, you become very cautious.

Job No 10. Description: Heavy 9ct yellow gold identity bracelet. Instructions: 'Please fit stronger type of fastener. This one has given continuous trouble'.

As no mention was made of an estimate and it being a very expensive bracelet, I assumed I could take extra time and trouble with this job. The existing fastener was a box snap and was made by cutting a link in half and fitting a tongue to one half and forming a box to take it in the other half. The idea, I think, was to make the fastener almost invisible, but the links were of such a size that the tongue had to be ridiculously small and consequently weak. A safety catch had been added to each side to compensate and had just about defeated the original object. The safety catches were loop-over ball type and had become very slack with use.

I decided that a ladder snap would be the best answer. Although it would be more than obvious, such a snap is very reliable if well made and does not require the help of a safety catch. If made with a back stop as indicated in Fig. 8-10, by soldering the hinge tube a short way in from the end, should the snap become accidently opened it will form a right angle and cannot easily unhook itself. In addition, if the distances between the rungs is only just sufficient to allow the foldover top to be threaded through, Fig. 8-11, there is even less chance of it coming completely apart because the hook of the tongue will tend to catch on the rung.

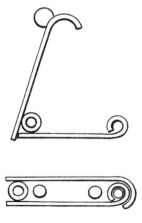

Fig 8.10 (Left) A ladder snap fastener with a back stop so that it does not open completely to release the bracelet if caught on something.

Fig 8.11 (Below) If adjacent rungs of the ladder nearly fill the space in the fastener, the chance of its opening completely accidentally are reduced even more.

The making of the snap is obvious and fairly straightforward. The ladder is made from one 'U' shaped piece of metal and the two rungs soldered into place. It makes the job easier and stronger if you drill holes through the sides of the 'U' to take the rungs because they will stay in place while the ladder is soldered on to the bracelet. A much sharper bend can be made in the two corners at the bottom of the 'U' if you file half way through the inside corners with the edge of a square file before bending them, then run solder into the corners afterwards.

File a flat on the end link of the bracelet sufficient to take all of the base of the ladder, Fig. 8-12. It then looks more integrated and less of an addition. The same is true of the snap end.

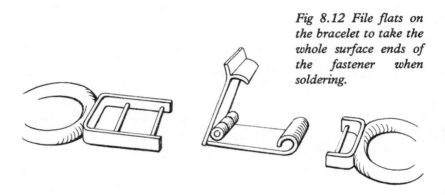

Fig 8.12 File flats on the bracelet to take the whole surface ends of the fastener when soldering.

The tube for the hinge should be as thick walled as possible because the rung of the ladder is in constant contact with it and wear will take place at that point.

The two ways of forming the tongue of the fastener are shown. The one with the tongue soldered on separately (Fig. 8-12) is easier to open and close but more likely to get knocked open accidently. The reverse is the case where the tongue is formed by bending the top flap into a hook (Fig. 8-10) but the small ball soldered to the top to enable it to be opened plays havoc with the thumbnail, but is almost impossible to knock open accidently. I chose it because it was a man's bracelet and men are not so particular about the condition of their nails as women, and a broken thumbnail is better than a lost bracelet!

Appendix 1

The Lathe

Not many jewellery workshops possess a metal turning lathe, so it must be considered a luxury. It is such a versatile machine, however, that it is difficult to do without it, once having become accustomed to one being available.

If you cannot afford a pendant drill a watchmaker's lathe that is too worn or inaccurate for a watchmaker can be picked up cheaply and makes a good substitute. Also it can tackle many jobs a pendant drill cannot. Its collets will take all the drills and burrs you will need to use and a small grinding wheel can be fitted for tool sharpening.

By glueing a coin centrally to one side of a 3 in (75 mm) plywood disc, the coin can be gripped in the step chuck and the disc rotated in the lathe. By glueing thin foam rubber and a circle of wet and dry emery paper to the plywood, opals and other small cabs can be repolished as described on page 000. Small felt discs are available which, when fitted on a suitable arbor and gripped in a colllet, will enable the final polish to be applied, using cerium oxide paste.

The tailstock is used mainly for holding a centre bit, but if you turn the knurled centre portion of an ordinary pin vice to fit the tailstock clamp (Fig. A1.1), you can fit drills into the pin vice and slide the tailstock along the bed. This enables you to drill holes dead-centre in any size disc held in a step chuck.

The watchmaker's lathe is built for such fine metal turning that it is not much use to a jeweller in that department. However, by using a needle file instead of a cutter, grooves and shapes can be formed on any diameter of wire that the collets will take. Examples of work for which this method is excellent are: making a new foot for a miniature cauldron and a new bone knob for a silver teapot lid.

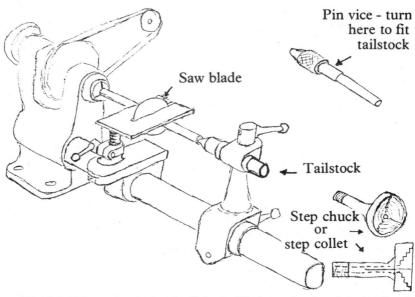

Fig. A1.1 The author's sketch of his modified watchmakers's lathe, fitted with circular saw.

The circular saw blade from a ring-cutting machine can be mounted on a brass arbor, gripped in a collet and supported by a centre bit in the tailstock as shown in Fig. A1.1. This will take the hard work out of many accurate sawing jobs and save a few piercing blades. A little brass saw table is made as shown. The round support that fits into the cross slide need only be soft soldered to the underside of the table.

The lathe will form the cut in a piece of shank wire needed to make a split shank (page 63) quickly and accurately, which is not always the case when a piercing saw is used. The blade must be frequently lubricated with bees or paraffin wax otherwise it will quickly lose its cutting edge.

Heavier Lathes

An instrument maker's lathe is a larger and heavier version of the watchmaker's lathe. Its greater centre height, self centering chucks and screw-operated cross slide enable it to tackle a much larger range of work. The little cap punching dies for the Pinfold machine could easily be made on one of these.

Such lathes are built for extreme precision work and are consequently very expensive and not many appear on the secondhand market. Cheaper alternatives are the various model maker's lathes. They come in a variety of designs and sizes from not much larger than a watchmaker's to cabinet-mounted ones that can swing a 10 in (25 cm) disc or turn a 3 ft-long (91 cm) bar.

The most versatile of them, from a jeweller's point of view, is the Austrian-made Unimat. It has a large range of accessories, including a flexible drive with a handpiece that can take the place of a pendant drill. The machine will only take up to 3-4 sq ft (2.8 - 3.7 sq m) of bench space.

When buying a secondhand lathe the main points to look for are:

1. Wear on the mandrel bearing. If these are solid bearings, they are usually adjustable. If the adjustment has been fully taken up, there is a fair chance the mandrel is worn as well.

2. Chips or grooves on the cross slide or tool rest is usually the result of one or the other having been driven into a rotating chuck. If this has happened a few times, the owner was very careless and may have treated other parts of the machine negligently. The result of this can be that the mandrel is out of alignment and anything turned on it will have a taper.

3. The bed should be free of dents or chips. If it has been used as an anvil at any time, the chances are that the saddle will not traverse the bed smoothly, and any turning done on it will be patchy and inaccurate.

A useful booklet for the potential lathe owner is *Using the Small Lathe*, by L. C. Mason, published by M.A.P. Technical Publications.

Appendix 2

Workshop Security

One only has to read the local newspapers or the police circulars to realise how important security is, and what a choice target a jeweller's workshop is, often tucked away in a back street where the rent and rates are more reasonable.

The most important item on the list of precautions is the safe. Any type of alarm depends for its effectiveness on someone taking notice of it - and doing something about it. Unless the system is wired direct to the police station it can be ineffective because an alarm bell is often ignored by the public long enough for a burglar to make his escape.

I know of one case where every door and window was effectively alarmed and the thieves dragged a large mattress into a side entry and made a hole in a 9-in brick wall under its cover. Had the owners of that firm not had the majority of the valuables in its care locked in a large safe, they would no doubt have customers as well as money.

It is very tempting on the grounds of economy to buy a secondhand safe, but if it is key-operated you will not usually know how many keys it had originally, who possessed them or whether any others have ben made. Maybe it is unlikely that anyone would keep a key with the intention of robbing it at a later date, but compare the cost of a new combination-locked safe with the cost of being robbed of several thousand pounds' worth of other people's jewellery. Even if you are covered by insurance, that will not cover you for the loss of confidence your customers will feel, or the time and trouble it will take to establish the value and ownership of every item taken. Moreover, you cannot insure for the sentimental value of wedding rings and engagement rings and that is often more important to their owners than their intrinsic value. For the sake of spending a few hundred pounds, you could be put out of business for a long time.

I have never had a safe that did not turn out to be too small for my requirements twelve months after I had acquired it. Inevitably there are times when you get a build-up of large items: trophies to have little shields attached to their bases, silver ornaments for repair, watches or masonic jewels in their original, bulky presentation cases, and you have to decide what to risk leaving out.

Another advantage of a large safe is the difficulty of moving it. One that you can manage to install yourself or with the help of a friend can be removed by someone else as easily.

Keys can be lost and they tend to wear holes in pockets very rapidly. There is little more annoying than to arrive at work and discover you have left your safe keys at home. A combination lock solves all these problems. You can set the combination yourself so that no-one else can know what it is, and you can change it at any time should the need arise.

Insurance companies will cover different makes of safe for different premiums, so if you intend asking for insurance cover it is as well to check with them before deciding which safe to buy.

Their degree of confidence in it will be a guide to its worth and effectiveness. You can have the help of their vast experience for the cost of a phone call.

If you cannot afford a proper alarm system, a red painted metal box fixed high on an outside wall with 'Burglar Alarm' professionally painted on it will be a precaution until you can - as long as you keep the secret to yourself! Often premises that are professionally alarmed have a dummy bell at the rear of the premises in case the burglar missed the one on the front or thought it only covered that side of the building.

DIY alarm kits are available and fitting one of these is better than having none at all. They are relatively cheap and easy to install and usually consist of a control box with an ignition type key and switch which contains the batteries and relays, and a block of terminals to take several circuits. There are magnetic switches for fitting to doors and vibrator switches for fitting to windows and indoor and outdoor bells or sirens. You can use floor pressure pads as well, but these are not usually suitable for a workshop or office adjoining a workshop because sharp snippet of metal can become embedded in them and cause a short circuit.

Wired alarm systems, unless thay are carried to extremes, can usually be bypassed by the enterprising crook. You can have a deadlock and a magnetic switch fitted to the door, but unless the whole of the door is criss-crossed with wires it is an easy matter to kick a panel out or cut a hole.

Permanently closed windows can be guarded by having a metal tape stuck across them which sets off the alarm if broken, or the vibration switches mentioned earlier glued to their centre; but opening windows will have to be guarded with a grid of aluminium tubes containing alarm wires which set off the alarm if the tubes are bent or broken. However, the tubes make window cleaning a contortionists' job.

The most convenient system is the infra-red alarm which fills the room with radio waves that are sensitive to movement or changes in temperature, thus acting as a fire alarm as well. With them, another vunerable spot - the ceiling - is covered as well. The alarm has to be set so that the minute hand on your electric clock or a visiting rat or the sun's rays will not set it off, but once set it is a very reliable and trouble-free system.

A final precaution is to get your keys registered. There are several firms that, for a very modest fee, will issue you with a little brass tag to attach to your key ring. Or it is a serial number which is also kept in their files along with your name and address. On the other side the finder is informed that he or she will recieve a reward if the keys are handed in to the nearest police station.

Appendix 3

Jewellers' Guide to Gemstone Handling

Explanation and Notes on Chart Sections

Section A

Hardness refers to the resistance of stones to being scratched. All steel tools may scratch stones with a hardness of 6 or less. The hard blue rubber wheels used to trim prongs during setting will scratch all stones except diamond. The softer grey pumice wheels should be used for coloured stones above the hardness of 5. Use no abrasive wheels with stones under 5 in hardness.

Toughness refers to the danger of stones being damaged by the various processes used in the manufacturing and handling of stone set jewellery. A rating of excellent to good means that the stone will be safe if reasonable care is exercised. A rating of fair to poor means that special care must be taken or the process avoided entirely.

Section B

Setting: These caution points apply to all setting jobs.
1. Any stone with a knife edge girdle is dangerous to set. Pressure of prongs should be only above or below the girdle edge, never directly against it.
2. Examine stones carefully with a loupe for cracks or flaws on or near the points where prongs might be pressed. Avoid excess pressure in tightening such stones. If stones are too transluscent, use a small torch to help spot flaws.

Section C

Polishing involves the use of abrasive powders.
1. Rouge is a very fine abrasive and may be used with all stone jewellery except pearls.
2. Tripoli will scratch or dull the polish of stones with a hardness of 5 or less.
3. Stones listed as poor should be set after jewellery has been prepared and polished.

Section D
Repairs and Sizing
1. Thorough cleaning of all jewellery needing repairs must be done.
2. Stones should be removed if repairs are required near the stone.
3. Stones which may be dyed or oiled will be damaged by such heat.
4. If repairs are made with stones set (as in sizing) be sure the stone has cooled before rinsing or pickling in acid. The centre of the stone stays hot longer than the outside and time must be allowed for it to cool. If you must rinse while the piece is still hot, then do it in hot water. The rule is *no fast temperature changes*.
5. On sizing jobs with the stones set, the stone may be protected by keeping it upside down in a water-filled bottle cap while soldering the bottom of the shank.

Section E
Boiling
1. Never put a coloured stone directly into boiling water. If the stone can take heat well, then put it in cold water and bring to the boil slowly.
2. Rinse in a hot water rinse if stone is still warm or in a warm water rinse if stone has cooled for a while. Again the rule is *no fast temperature changes*.
3. Do not boil rubies or emeralds. Many of these are 'oiled' and they will lose colour if boiled. Such stones should be removed before the jewellery is boiled and reset afterwards.
4. When cleaning such jewellery pieces, use a soft brush in lukewarm water with a mild soap or detergent.

Section F
Steaming
1. Do not steam while stone is cold. Rinse first in warm water, not hot.
2. When steaming do not hold stone with tweezers. Hold only the mounting, not the stone.

Section G
Ultrasonic
1. Solution should be kept warm if used as a cleaner after polishing.
2. Stones which have been heat treated are usually under strain and may crack in the ultrasonic process. Such stones are listed as poor and should be cleaned as listed under Section E4.

Section H
Acids
1. Acids are used in the pickling and plating processes. Again avoid fast temperature changes. Keep plating baths warm and rinse with warm water after using.
2. Do not use with stones which are organic or dyed. Stones listed as poor will be harmed by acids. They should be removed before repairing jewellery in which they are set.
3. Porous stones are also affected by acids. Examples are turquoise, malachite, azurite, and shell cameos.

STONE	HARDNESS & TOUGHNESS (read section A)	REACTION TO SETTING (read section B)	REACTION TO POLISHING (read section C)	REACTION TO SIZING & REPAIRS WHICH REQUIRE TORCH (read section D)	REACTION TO BOILING (read section E)
DIAMOND	H 10 T good	very good	excellent	good	excellent
RUBY AND SAPPHIRE (Corundum)	H 9 T very good	very good	excellent	Ruby-good Sapphires may lose colour when heated	good
CATSEYE & ALEXANDRITE (chrysoberyl)	H 8½ T very good	very good	excellent	good-fair; remove if repairs are made near stone	good
SPINEL	H 8 T good-fair	very good-fair	very good	good-fair; remove if repairs are made near stone	good-fair
EMERALD (beryl)	H 7½-8 T poor	poor; stones usually flawed and under strain	fair; do not apply heavy pressure	poor; stones should never be heated	poor; should be cleaned in lukewarm water only
PRECIOUS TOPAZ	H 8 T poor	fair-poor; take care stone cleaves easily	good	poor; stones may crack or lose colour	poor
AQUAMARINE (beryl)	H 7½-8 T good-fair	good-fair	good	poor; stone may change colour with heat	fair-poor; avoid fast temperature changes

STONE	HARDNESS & TOUGHNESS (read section A)	REACTION TO SETTING (read section B)	REACTION TO POLISHING (read section C)	REACTION TO SIZING & REPAIRS WHICH REQUIRE TORCH (read section D)	REACTION TO BOILING (read section E)
TOURMALINE	H 7-7½ / T good-fair	good-fair	good	fair-poor	fair
GARNET incl. RHODOLITE & TSAVORITE	H 6½-7½ / T good-fair	good-fair; flawed stones are under strain	good	fair-poor; play safe, remove expensive stone before repair	fair-poor
RUTILE & FABULITE (synthetic)	H 6½-7 / T poor-very poor	very poor; will take very little pressure	very poor, use very light pressure or set after polishing	very poor; stones will crack with heat	poor, stone may crack
AMETHYST & CITRINE (quartz)	H 6½-7 / T good	good	good	fair; colour may change with heat	fair
PERIDOT	H 6½-7 / T poor-very poor	poor; facet edges chip easily	poor	very poor, remove stone before repairs or sizing are made	poor; avoid extreme temperatures
TANZANITE (zoisite)	H 6½ / T poor	poor	fair (avoid heavy pressure)	very poor; remove before repairs are made	poor
JADEITE & NEPHRITE (jade)	H 6-7 / T excel.	excellent	fair; tripoli may damage polish on stone. Use only rouge	poor, no repairs near stone	good; heat may discolour dyed material

STONE	HARDNESS & TOUGHNESS (read section A)	REACTION TO SETTING (read section B)	REACTION TO POLISHING (read section C)	REACTION TO SIZING & REPAIRS WHICH REQUIRE TORCH (read section D)	REACTION TO BOILING (read section E)
KUNZITE & HIDDENITE (spodumene)	H 6-7 T very poor	poor	fair	poor, stones will lose colour	poor; may crack if boiled
ZIRCON	H 6-6½ T poor	poor	fair	poor	poor
MOONSTONE (feldspar)	H 6-6½ T fair-poor	good-fair	good-fair	poor	poor
OPAL - Also doublets & triplets	H 5½-6½ T very poor	poor	poor (avoid heavy pressure)	very poor; remove before repairs are made	poor, boiling will crack stone, triplets separate
HEMATITE	H 5-6½ T good-fair	good-fair	good-fair	poor	good
TURQUOISE	H 5-6 T good-poor	fair	fair	very poor; stone will explode with heat	poor; may lose colour
LAPIS LAZULI (lazurite)	H 5-6 T fair-poor	fair	fair- poor; tripoli will harm polish on stone	poor	fair-poor; some dyed stones will lose colour

STONE	HARDNESS & TOUGHNESS (read section A)	REACTION TO SETTING (read section B)	REACTION TO POLISHING (read section C)	REACTION TO SIZING & REPAIRS WHICH REQUIRE TORCH (read section D)	REACTION TO BOILING (read section E)
SHELL CAMEO	H 3½ T poor	poor, will crack with excess pressure	poor; polish jewellery lightly with very little pressure	cannot take heat of repair. Will show burn marks	Colour will fade if boiled
CORAL	H 3-4 T good-poor	good	poor, use rouge only	very poor; remove stone before repair	poor; may lose colour
PEARLS & MABES	H 2½-4½ T fair-poor	fair; mabes take pressure poorly	poor;will affect lustre badly	poor; pearls will burn	poor; may lose colour tint, Mabes separate
IVORY	H 2½-3 T fair	fair	fair-poor, use light pressure	poor; heat will cause stone to shrink	fair-poor; dyed pieces may lose colour
AMBER	H 2-2½ T poor	very poor; will scratch easily	poor	very poor; stone will melt or burn	very poor, do not boil

STONE	REACTION TO STEAMING (read Section F)	REACTION TO ULTRASONIC (read Section G)	REACTION TO ACIDS, PICKLING & PLATING (read Section H)	COMMENTS (add your own comments based upon your own experience)
DIAMOND	excellent	excellent	excellent	
RUBY AND SAPPHIRE (Corundum)	good	good	good	watch for oiled stones. Do not heat
CATSEYE & ALEXANDRITE (chrysoberyl)	good	good	good	
SPINEL	good	good	good	
EMERALD (beryl)	poor	fair	poor; stones may crack or lose oil if solutions are too hot	avoid all heat; Chatham and Gilson synthetics react the same as natural stones
PRECIOUS TOPAZ	poor	fair	good	any heating may discolour or crack stone
AQUAMARINE (beryl)	fair	fair	good	

STONE	REACTION TO STEAMING (read Section F)	REACTION TO ULTRASONIC (read Section G)	REACTION TO ACIDS, PICKLING & PLATING (read Section H)	COMMENTS (add your own comments based upon your own experience)
TOURMALINE	fair	good	good-fair	may change colour with heat during repairs
GARNET incl. RHODOLITE & TSAVORITE	fair	good	fair-poor; acids may affect polish on stone	
RUTILE & FABULITE (synthetic)	poor	fair-poor	fair	reacts poorly under heat and pressure
AMETHYST & CITRINE (quartz)	fair	good	good-fair	
PERIDOT	fair-poor	fair	poor	should not get much heat or pressure
TANZANITE (zoisite)	poor	poor	fair	will not take much heat or pressure
JADEITE & NEPHRITE (jade)	good	good	poor; acid will affect polish on stone	

STONE	REACTION TO STEAMING (read Section F)	REACTION TO ULTRASONIC (read Section G)	REACTION TO ACIDS, PICKLING & PLATING (read Section H)	COMMENTS (add your own comments based upon your own experience)
KUNZITE & HIDDENITE (spodumene)	poor	fair	fair	heat may fade colour
ZIRCON	poor	fair	fair	does not take heat well
MOONSTONE (feldspar)	fair	fair	fair-poor	
OPAL - Also doublets & triplets	poor	fair-poor	poor	Opals should be examined by shining a light through the stone to see if there are cracks. Do not process cracked stones
HEMATITE	good	good	poor; acids attack stones	
TURQUOISE	fair	fair-poor	very poor; will dissolve in acids	takes heat and pressure poorly. Colour may fade in untreated stones
LAPIS LAZULI (lazurite)	good	good-fair	poor; will change-colour. Acid will attack Pyrite & Calcite inclusions	many lapis are dyed. Colours may change with heat or acids

STONE	REACTION TO STEAMING (read Section F)	REACTION TO ULTRASONIC (read Section G)	REACTION TO ACIDS, PICKLING & PLATING (read Section H)	COMMENTS (add your own comments based upon your own experience)
SHELL CAMEO	fair-poor	fair	very poor; will dissolve in acids	Cameos made of shell are very delicate and will not take much heat or pressure
CORAL	fair	fair	very poor; will dissolve in acids	much coral is dyed and will be affected by heat
PEARLS & MABES	fair	fair	very poor; will dissolve in acids	watch for spot in nacre which may be hollow underneath
IVORY	good	fair	fair	many imitations available, all react differently
AMBER	poor-fair	poor	very poor; will dissolve in acids	many imitations will react the same

Index

Numbers in italics (thus *67*) refer to illustrations on pages shown

189